LEISURE

'The object of Tony Blackshaw's learned, erudite study is, in his own words, "the variety and ambiguity of actual human experience"; yet the purpose of his study is not "tidying-up the confusion" or "setting out what leisure *should* mean", but revealing, laying bare and explaining that dense fog of complexity which we daily confront and daily, with little success, try to find our own trail through. In reaching that objective, he does enormous service to all among us bold and adventurous enough to admit that such a trail is to be blazed, not found …'

Zygmunt Bauman *Professor Emeritus at the Universities of Leeds, UK, and Warsaw, Poland*

No single introductory book has until now captured the range of thought appropriate for scrutinizing the idea of leisure. Beginning with a discussion of expressions in classical thought, etymological definitions and key leisure studies concepts, Blackshaw suggests that the idea abounds with ambivalence, which is unlikely ever to be resolved.

After analysing the rise and fall of modern leisure patterns, the emphasis shifts from the historical to the sociological and the author identifies and critically discusses the key modernist and postmodernist perspectives. Drawing on the idea that leisure studies is a 'language game', Blackshaw subsequently offers his own original theory of liquid leisure which asks some key questions about the present and the future of leisure in people's lives, as well as what implications it has for individuals' abilities to embrace the opportunity for an authentic existence that is both magical and moral.

Leisure is an essential purchase for undergraduate and postgraduate students, researchers and academics in the fields of Sociology of Leisure, Sports and Leisure Studies, and Popular Culture.

Tony Blackshaw teaches Social and Cultural Studies in Sport and Leisure at Sheffield Hallam University. He is the author of numerous articles and books on leisure including, *The Sage Dictionary of Leisure Studies* (2009) and *Leisure Life: Myth, Masculinity and Modernity* (2003).

KEY IDEAS

Series Editor: PETER HAMILTON

Designed to compliment the successful *Key Sociologists*, this series covers the main concepts, issues, debates, and controversies in sociology and the social sciences. The series aims to provide authoritative essays on central topics of social science, such as community, power, work, sexuality, inequality, benefits and ideology, class, family, etc. Books adopt a strong 'individual' line, as critical essays rather than literature surveys, offering lively and original treatments of their subject matter. The books will be useful to students and teachers of sociology, political science, economics, psychology, philosophy, and geography.

LEISURE

Tony Blackshaw

Routledge
Taylor & Francis Group

LONDON AND NEW YORK

First published 2010
by Routledge
2 Park Square, Milton Park, Abingdon, Oxon, OX14 4RN

Simultaneously published in the USA and Canada
by Routledge
270 Madison Avenue, New York, NY 10016

Routledge is an imprint of the Taylor & Francis Group, an informa business

Typeset in Garamond and Scala by Swales & Willis Ltd, Exeter, Devon
Printed and bound in !   by Bhavish Graphics.

British Library Cataloguing in Publication Data
A catalogue record for this book is available from the British Library

Library of Congress Cataloging in Publication Data

Blackshaw, Tony, 1960-
Leisure / Tony Blackshaw.
p. cm.
Includes bibliographical references.
1. Leisure. I. Title.
GV14.B53 2010
790.1 – dc22
2009036854

ISBN10: 0–415–43027–5

ISBN13: 978–0–415–43027–2

CONTENTS

ACKNOWLEDGEMENTS

Many of the ideas and arguments relating to the core concepts in leisure studies developed in this book made their first appearance in *The Sage Dictionary of Leisure Studies* and I would like to acknowledge my gratitude to Sage Publications for supporting my use of them in this revised way.

INTRODUCTION

The central aim of this book is to present its readers with a brief but critical interpretation of the idea of modern leisure. The point of departure for this assessment, written at my own leisure – *skholē*, otherwise known as 'the free time, freed from the urgencies of the world, that allows a free and liberated relation to those urgencies and to the world' (Bourdieu, 2000: 1), obviously played a key part, but so also did idleness – is the recognition that this idea is currently in transition as a result of some profound social, cultural, economic and political changes. Such an effort might, to some, seem faintly perverse since the study of leisure is usually left to the 'leisure studies' perspective – the discursive formation or conceptual field which until quite recently took on none of the difficulty of defining that goes with its object of study – for whom scholarly work is 'mostly atheoretical, sees and researches leisure as though it were a male or unisex phenomenon, which utilizes large scale surveys and often separates leisure from its wider context' (Deem, 1986: 8). 'Leisure studies' enjoyed a modicum of prominence, particularly in Australasia, North America and the United Kingdom, for a brief period from the late 1960s until the mid-1980s, when its star started to wane.

This decline has been mirrored in interest in the idea itself and today the study of leisure has by and large dropped off the curriculum at most universities. I conjecture that if a poll were conducted among students today regarding the popularity of the various topics in the social sciences, 'leisure' would come very low down the list in terms of perceived importance and interest. Why? One of the reasons for this, of course, is that as Hugh Cunningham rightly points out, the idea of "leisure" is an abstraction from everyday experience: 'People talk about concrete, discrete activities – going to the pub, or the races, or choir practice, watching television, or playing football – not about "leisure"' (1980: 13). From my own dealings with students today, though, I'd hazard a guess that 'leisure' carries no weight since it is an idea which to them feels vaguely 'uncool'. You might speculate that – unlike, say, sport or crime, for example – it is not very good at dramatizing its sense of being an outsider, which is exactly the dynamic of cool (as we shall see in Chapter 6 of this book, this concept is crucial for understanding leisure today). Just as likely, I'd also speculate that it is simply the case that leisure studies – in common with recreation studies – have lost their lustre. Whichever argument is the most accurate, the truth is that the idea of 'leisure' no longer burns brightly in the lives of students, because it does not have within its grasp an overarching narrative of sufficient power, simplicity and wide appeal to compete with the other lures of lives made to the measure of *individualization*, which today is *the* shaping force in the narrative of human existence.

There is also of course a long tradition within the social sciences of casting doubt upon leisure's conceptual credentials. Notwithstanding the important work of a small number of leisure scholars, Ken Roberts (1970; 1978; 1981; 1983; 1999), Rosemary Deem (1986), John Clarke and Chas Critcher (1985), Peter Bramham (Haywood *et al.*, 1995; 2006) and John Spink (1994; Haywood *et al.*, 1995) in the UK, but especially the work of Chris Rojek (1985; 1995; 2000; 2005; 2010) in sociology, leisure's star has never really waxed, and where it stands today in the pecking order of key ideas is fairly easy to identify. Some might say that the status of any key idea depends on too many variables and fluctuates too widely for anyone to judge it with assurance on any lasting basis. This observation, notwithstanding, to borrow an analogy from Richard Carpenter (1976), I'd say that conceptual status operates a lot like stock-market logic in which a vast number of imponderables – not least the arrogances of snobbery, the vagaries of fashion and the bandwagon attitude where people like to get their money on a good thing – play a surreal and incalculable part. At the present time, 'community', 'identity', 'social capital' and 'sport' are the leaders, blue-chip ideas with sustained growth; 'class', 'culture' and 'gender' are still thought of as solid investments, like the government bonds used to bail out failing banks; 'globalization', 'lifestyle', 'media' and 'tourism' (the oldest of the new key ideas) are bullish; 'postmodernity', whose star was only a short time ago so bright that it hurt the eyes, is a bit bearish; and 'leisure' continues selling short.

This stock-market analogy is not entirely satisfactory since many of the matters surrounding the idea of leisure are currently being elaborated in introductory books about 'health and wellbeing', 'sport' and 'tourism'. The forms that these introductions tend to take, however, often evade theory in favour of facts and/or separate their topics from the wider social, economic, cultural and political context in which they occur. As for the term itself, 'leisure' is invariably associated with free time and/or used to refer to the opportunities presented by free time. In these definitions, life is compartmentalized and leisure lives constitute just another compartment. The idea of 'leisure' implies watching television, going to the pub on a Friday night, playing golf at the weekend and so on, but not paid work or dealing with household responsibilities. This understanding would at first glance seem unavoidable since what we understand as leisure today was produced by the major societal upheavals (the topic of Chapter 3 in this book) that led to the advent of modernity, which saw the substitution of a patterned and ordered society for the traditional world of community and with this its separation from work.

Yet this kind of definition hardly accounts for the complexity and the conceptual scope of the idea. Used in this way, as the anti-thesis of work, leisure is a good example of the philosopher Ludwig Wittgenstein's admonition that human thought is often held prisoner by static images. A closer look reveals that there is in our present age a long standing (in contemporary terms at least) societal shift to a pouring-away 'liquid' modernity (Bauman, 2000a), a global world that is underpatterned rather than patterned, disorganized rather than ordered, in which we once again see a blurring of the boundaries that until quite recently separated self-contained areas of modern life: 'leisure' from 'education', 'home' from 'work', 'work' from 'leisure', 'leisure from work', and all the rest besides.

The two following examples illustrate this argument. In his book *The Labour of Leisure: the Culture of Free Time* (2010), Chris Rojek argues that where once upon a time attaining just the right amount of competence, relevance and credibility was essential to be regarded as a valued worker, it is these very same attributes that are today what enables us to develop and nourish meaningful leisure lives. A good example of the reverse process is the way in which the intelligent hand of capitalism has recently appropriated four key attributes from the leisure sphere: immediacy, playfulness, subjectivity and performativity, as attributes of entrepreneurship in the workplace (Bauman, 2008a: 126). The upshot of these de-differentiating tendencies is that just as 'work' has become 'leisure-like', 'leisure' has become 'work-like'. What this also suggests that there might be many more inexplicable things that people do in their 'leisure' than we think, which do not obey rational logic, the way that dreams do not follow the logic of stories. What this would seem to suggest is that life today is consistent only in its inconsistencies; what this means is that if leisure – what

I call 'liquid leisure' – is not impossible to describe in words, it is perhaps more difficult than it was once supposed.

These processes of de-differentiation have been accompanied by some other key changes in leisure. At the beginning of the 1970s, in attempting to define leisure, Ken Roberts wrote about the Big Five leisure pursuits: gambling; sex; alcohol; television; and annual holidays. As Critcher and Bramham (2004: 45) point out, each of these has held its own, but what they perhaps underestimate is the extent to which the world of leisure has changed over the last 30 years. To the Big Five has also been added the Big Two of drug taking and shopping (and the credit that accompanies it), but also the rewiring of traditional leisure activities and pursuits – cybersex, digital gaming, celebrating watching and social networking – through information technology and the internet. On top of this, in the UK, many pools fillers now play the national lottery; sex tourism is a global problem and barebacking or unprotected anal intercourse in episodic sexual encounters among same-sex attracted men is apparently a global phenomenon (Ridge, 2004); an astonishing 52 pubs in the UK are closing every week (O'Connor, 2009), at the same time many drink themselves into oblivion inside the comfort of their own homes; the 28 million viewers (half the population) in the UK in 1977 who watched the Mike Yarwood and the Morecambe and Wise comedy Christmas specials telling them jokes about the sameness of the ways that they lived have now fragmented into variegated watchers of global distributed 'reality' television shows in all their variety – *Strictly Come Dancing*, *Big Brother*, *Who Do You Think You Are?*, *The Jerry Springer Show*, and all the rest – presented to them by and/or 'starring' celebrities; while annual package holidays in Spain have been replaced by short trips to the seaside and city breaks with budget airlines. And to boot, in less than 30 years 'a nation of shopkeepers' has been turned, not so much into 'a nation of shoppers' (Haywood *et al.*, 1995), as into one of lemming-like consumers – or so it would seem.

Looking at these shifts in the processes of societal modernization we also find that the contemporary 'liquid' world is one of constant 'disembedding' and 're-embedding' – as the sociologist Anthony Giddens would say – where men and women, freed from the shackles of the imagined 'social contract' that accompanied the virtues and the habitats of a 'solid' modern society based on industrial production (which cast them 'ready-made' through their rank in the social class and gender hierarchies), have become the agents of their own destinies. Indeed, during the decades from the 1970s onwards men and women were increasingly becoming newly dislocated (or at least semi-assimilated) in the world and as a result the normative institutions associated with modern societies have been transformed.

Let us consider the influence of paid work on our leisure once again. There is no doubting the fact that it still has a considerable bearing on our leisure opportunities and choices, but particularly over the last 20 years there has been a clear shift in what work means to us as individuals. Today it is the pursuit of pleasure and happiness – much more than work – that appears to shape our sense of ourselves. What this also means is that the most important category in modern life today is no longer what we have to do (read: necessity), but what we want to do (read: freedom) with the contingency that entails. Life today is about people trying to find out what matters most to them, and then to do it – especially in their free time. Whether this is a realistic aspiration or not is beside the point.

What all of this suggests is that in order to develop a contemporary interpretation of leisure we must not only break with the convention of seeing it as merely a residual category of work (as we shall see in the next chapter, this is not a new endeavour), but also re-think it in nearly every other respect (this is new). This is because the questions concerning leisure and freedom not only revolve around individualization, consumerism and the pursuit of pleasure and happiness, but they are also concerned with a whole host of other issues – identity, community, responsibility, performativity, love, anxiety, fear, ontological and existential insecurity, the search for meaning, authenticity and so on – that dominate modern life today.

This is very different from saying that what has previously been written about leisure is unimportant. Rather what is being suggested is that much that was written about leisure under the auspices of leisure studies scholarship can sometimes be a barrier in preventing imaginative engagement with the different social, cultural, economic and political conditions that are the mark of 'liquid' modernity. What this means is that in trying to get to grips with leisure today we are in the position of having to deal with, a whole family of concepts which increasingly feel like the ghosts that haven't quite died – what the sociologist Ulrich Beck (2002) calls death-in-life zombie categories – lingering around a discursive formation that today only gives them a fitful and uncertain sense of still belonging to its world (Blackshaw, 2009a). A zombie category is a concept which is to all intents and purposes dead, but has been given a futile pseudo-life because it is being kept in use by those who really should know better. There is a sense in which all concepts are zombie categories. However, there is a tendency, especially among leisure scholars, to overlook the fact that some of leisure's family members, especially those developed under the aegis of 1970s and 1980s leisure studies have (just like leisure itself) been transformed by more recent societal changes and technological advances, in the process becoming grey areas of knowledge that have lost their former explanatory power. Today the leisure family is only consistent in its inconsistencies. It is against this background that the present study should be seen.

To keep up the family metaphor, what I am also proposing is that leisure must be interpreted pragmatically rather than definitively. With respect to this idea, reference must be made to Wittgenstein's (1967) idea of 'language games'. Wittgenstein knew that metaphors are important to clarifying understanding, not only because they use language in magical and enlivening ways, but also because they are edifying and enlightening. To this end his idea of 'language games' is concerned with the way in which words can only be properly understood in the context of their use. What this suggests for the purposes of the current study is that it is a mistake to extract words as they are used in the study of leisure out of the context of their 'natural home' and move them into the very different framework of a broader intellectual argument. In Wittgenstein's view, such a shift requires that the same meaning cannot be maintained throughout for these central terms when they are moved out of their home territory. What this suggests is that we might not be able to define leisure so accurately as to uncover its 'real' meaning, but we might try to understand it in terms of its 'family resemblances' and their own internal practices and rules, even if we believe that the very request to define the idea in a definitive way is a mistake. In other words, we shouldn't be asking after the *meaning* and the *purposes* of leisure, but should instead be asking after its *use*. Our task should be to clarify its contingencies and the ways in which the idea is used in different leisure situations rather than trying to pin it down to some absolute meaning.

What Wittgenstein's invocation of this conceptual schema suggests is that language doesn't so much represent the world – it is not answerable to some already existing reality – rather, it is a tool that we use to assign sense to things. Language is only meaningful because it is public and the ways in which we use it in particular contexts, where there are right and wrong ways of using it. What this tells us is that language use in leisure studies is proscribed by the rules of its own 'language game'. This last observation, notwithstanding, what we commonly associated with 'leisure', takes on different guises in different contexts – social and cultural as well as historical – and it is often difficult to separate it from other concepts – as we have already seen, especially work. It is often the case that we do work in our leisure time; it doesn't stop being work, but it is work of another kind. As the pragmatist philosopher Richard Rorty might have put it, the beauty of Wittgenstein's notion of 'family resemblances' is that it offers us a pragmatic way of accounting for similarities between different things in the world of leisure without supposing that there is some higher order of reality occupied by ontologically superior concepts. To reiterate, it is also particularly useful for asking after the use of leisure (as we shall see in Chapter 2) since its family members do not all have something in common with each other. The challenge this poses us with, however, is that we must make the application of our own conceptual schema clear by thinking it through, which means pulling together the major themes as well as the diaphanous threads connecting all leisure's family members. If we do this then our understanding of this key idea will become much clearer.

Such a conceptual schema will be like Plato's cave, in that it will give us only a partial and distorted view of reality, but we need this to cultivate a way of thinking about leisure which is critical, discursive and reflective. As the philosopher Martin Heidegger once said, one of the marks of being human is that we can think, in the sense that we possess the ability to do so. However, this possibility is no guarantee that we are capable of thinking critically. According to Zygmunt Bauman, the main reason why thinking can't be guaranteed is because we tend to get bogged down in our daily routines, to the extent that 'we hardly ever pause to think about the meaning of what we have gone through: even less often have we the opportunity to compare our private experience with the fate of others, to the *social* in the *individual*, the *general* in the *particular*' (Bauman, 1990: 10).

As Bauman points out, this is precisely what *thinking sociologically* can do for us. It is its distinctive sensibility that enables us to locate our own experiences within a broader historical and social context. For Bauman, as for C. Wright Mills, the sociologist who coined the term the *sociological imagination*, *thinking sociologically* enables us to distinguish between our own 'personal troubles' and 'public issues' (Mills, 1959), or more pointedly, to begin to conceptualize the relationship between the problem of own individual experiences and broader processes of social continuity and change.

What *thinking sociologically* suggests is that to be scholars good at our job, we not only need to understand what is going on in our own lives, but we must also take a *keen* interest in what is going on in the lives of other people. This entails temporarily shedding our own identities and suspending our own judgements in order that we can try to *feel* and *think* how other people *feel* and *think*, so that we can suitably identify and try to understand what hopes and fears prompt their lives. As the Turkish novelist Orhan Pamuk (2005) suggests, it is by using our imaginations in this way that we are also able to free ourselves from our own identities and in the process set ourselves free – as we shall see, debates about freedom are crucial to understanding leisure. This is also the reason why it is not really a matter of any great importance what we call the approach to the study of the subject we are about to explore. What matters more is the mind-set with which we approach this study of leisure, which will help us better understand what it means for individuals and society today.

When I was a student at the end of the 1980s we were introduced to the idea by breaking it down into its four key dimensions (Haywood *et al.*, 1995) – leisure as *residual time*, leisure as *activities*, identifying leisure by its social, cultural, political and economic *functions* and leisure as *freedom* – accompanied with the proviso that it is also more than the sum of its parts. This approach exposed me to talking across disciplinary boundaries, whereby it is possible to broach numerous other big subjects. What we have in this book is an analogous approach that extends the invitation of sociology in attempting to account for the phenomenon of leisure by operating on an 'indisciplinary' basis (Rancière, 2008), which is not only a matter of going above and beyond the call of duty of sociology as we normally understand it, but also breaking with it. In this way, this book rejects the pre-ordained distribution of academic territory which normally decides who is qualified to speak about what. Instead, it moves outside of the boundaries of the discipline of 'sociology', setting itself free by subordinating the false divisions between sociology, psychology, philosophy, history and so on to the educated imagination, which affects the whole person rather than just training the mind, bringing with it social and moral development that leads to the discovery that the imaginative world and the world around us are different worlds, and that the imaginative world *is more important* (Frye, 1963).

Indeed, my foremost aim in this book is to give the big picture vitality of leisure through abundance of detail, telling its story in terms of theory, but importantly also in the ways that people make use of leisure in their everyday lives. There are at least four reasons for finding the study of leisure compelling. First, there is the way in which leisure has adapted to the changed and always changing circumstances of modernity. The current 'liquid' trajectory of modernity is perhaps more complicated than that of any other period and trying to understand modernity's changed conventions through the idea of leisure is for this author fascinating. Second, and related to the last point, there is the challenge it presents to us to try and understand the world from the perspective of men and women themselves rather than just from an academic standpoint. Third, in its many manifestations leisure reminds us of the thrilling event that human subjectivity is and the infinite playfulness of the human mind. Finally, the study of leisure is exciting because it is infinitely variable, acquiring a new identity in the mind of every new participant. This is because it is always in both the intimate world of private life and the public world of culture and subject to the ever-changing human landscape in which it moves.

To achieve this discursive level of understanding, what follows is broken down into three parts. This is a divided book, in that it comprises three thirds of a different complexion, but these parts are complementary. In the first of these parts we shall attempt to characterize the idea of leisure in general. If we are to make sense of what I call liquid modern leisure in the final part of the book, we must identify its early modern origins.

This is no mean task since it is not always clear what the idea means or implies. Implicit to the discussions developed in the two chapters that make up Part I: Foundations is the question of what it is to raise questions about leisure. What is leisure? What does a study of leisure include and what does it exclude? As we shall see, some of these questions are much easier to answer than others. One might ask: should the idea incorporate work? Most people would answer this question with an unequivocal 'yes' since both work and leisure are braided in our experience and the latter without the former is unthinkable. But what if it turns out that the 'leisure' under discussion is deviant or abnormal, and which involves violence, sadistic behaviour, abuse and other violations of human or animal rights? The answer to this kind of question is less clear cut. As we shall see, in Chapter 2, in leisure studies there is an 'ethical' divide about whether or not such nasty activities should be classified as leisure.

This should come as no surprise since as we have already seen the idea of leisure is always used in accordance with 'language games' of the various everyday situations in which we find ourselves. What this means is that Part I will certainly not provide readers with any precise once and for all definition of leisure, but read cumulatively it will provide them with a set of 'family resemblances' for beginning to understand the various and often contested meanings of leisure in the ever-shifting sea of change that is modern existence.

As its title suggests Part II is about leisure in historical and social thought. Chapter 3 is about the history of leisure. I am not qualified to offer a definitive discussion of the history of leisure. Even if I was, such a history would amount to a compendium of fits and starts, as Peter Borsay's (2006) version attests, a fascinating record that would be impossible to detail in such a short book as this one. What is provided here is not a history of leisure as such. It is merely a thumbnail sketch, a social theory of history, a historicization of the past to be precise, preceded by a brief survey of the various histories that have already been written about the critical factors leading to the emergence of modern leisure. Faced with the task of developing a critique that avoids superficiality, the history of events pertaining to the emergence of modern leisure is kept to the minimum necessary, for the focus of this chapter is primarily concerned with the antecedents leading to the substitution of modernity for pre-modern traditional society, particularly the religious changes associated with the post-Reformation period, the Enlightenment, the societal drift towards individualization and the rise of capitalism and an industrial society based on social class differences. It will be suggested that what we find from the seventeenth century onwards is the co-existence of two modernizing leisure trends: the cold comfort of compensatory leisure against the grim Protestant work ethic and warm communal togetherness of popular culture pastimes against cold lonely individualism.

It is clear from this last observation that this book focuses almost entirely on modern leisure. To this extent it is interested not in leisure as a thing in itself, which typifies leisure studies, but the ways in which people *experience* leisure and its *social meaning*. Chapter 4 is thus concerned with the ways in which leisure has customarily been analysed as a social phenomenon. The sociology of leisure has been dominated by theories and counter-theories concerned with social class, gender and 'race' and it is these three topics that provide the major focus of this chapter. These three concepts also provide the basis of the critique developed in the second part of the chapter, which makes the controversial argument that if our lives are not completely free of their social class, gender and ethnic statuses, and that a democratic deficit continues to bedevil the leisure opportunities of some, it is an inescapable fact that the Western world is far less class-ridden, sexist and racist than it was a generation ago, and that by now these previously 'solid' markers of identity and difference are much more fluid and permeable than they were in the not too distant past. One of the upshots of this is that most people no longer (if they ever did) perceive their leisure lives through the prisms of 'class', 'gender', or even their ethnicity. To be modern today is to know our lives have a more in-between, DIY ready-made feel about them, and to this extent that they are better understood as *individualized* existences.

This view is implicit to understanding postmodern leisure in Chapter 5, which runs quite contrary to the structural accounts discussed in Chapter 4. 'Real' life does not show such theoretical symmetries, the postmodern imagination suggests, form is always imposed on life's fragments. From the perspective of the postmodern imagination the exact truth as to material fact ceases to be of importance in understanding leisure, and what is important are the things regarded as less important in structuralist accounts: individualization, contingency, freedom, nostalgia, pleasure, risk, hedonism, fantasy, happiness, desire, pastiche, irony, hyperreality, and much else besides. It is these concepts that form the basis of Chris Rojek's (1995) seminal work on postmodern leisure, which provides the starting point for the discussion in this chapter. After outlining what is meant by the terms postmodernism and postmodernity and discussing what implications the emergence of such a sensibility and a sociality have for understanding leisure, the chapter explores what happens when the postmodern imagination becomes integral to sociological method. The chapter closes with a discussion of straw target criticisms of 'postmodernism' and a counter response.

In Part III: Towards a Theory of Liquid Leisure I offer my own theory of leisure which is linked to the following question: what becomes of leisure when the pursuit of pleasure and happiness are the twin aims of human existence? The two chapters which form the basis of my thesis are written as a critical response to Chris Rojek's (2010) thesis in his new book *The Labour of Leisure*, which argues in a nutshell that on the one hand consumption is *not* leisure and on the other that leisure is best understood as *skholē*. In Chapter 6, the first part of Rojek's thesis is critically assessed by way of a critical discussion of the efficacy of Ritzer's (1993; 2003) McDonaldization thesis, which is juxtaposed with my own alternative IKEAization thesis. Chapter 7 answers the question of what leisure is if it is not freedom by arguing that in liquid modernity it has become instead hermeneutical, or more and more meaning.

Part I

FOUNDATIONS

1

THE IDEA OF LEISURE

As we saw in the introduction the study of modern leisure is usually left to 'leisure studies'. In their accounts, its roots tend to be in individual choice, freedom and self-determination (Rojek, 2005; 2010). As for the term itself, 'modern leisure' is standardly defined as a 'relatively self-determined activity-experience that falls into one's economically free-time roles, that is seen as leisure by participants, that is psychologically pleasant in anticipation and recollection, that potentially covers the whole range of commitment and intensity, that contains characteristic norms and constraints, and that provides opportunities for recreation, personal growth and service to others' (Kaplan, 1975: 26).

This kind of definition elicits an understanding of leisure in modern thought, but the idea is also among the oldest in the history of ideas, and among the most fundamental. The Greeks argued that leisure is the very basis of culture (Pieper, 1998: 1948). As Aristotle saw it, the

> first principle of all action is leisure ... leisure of itself gives pleasure, happiness and enjoyment of life, which are experienced, not by the busy man, but by those who have leisure. For he who is occupied has in view some end which his has not attained; but happiness is an end, since all men deem it to be accompanied with pleasure and not pain. This pleasure, however, is rewarded differently by different persons, and varies according to the habit of the individual.
>
> (quoted in Shivers and deLisle, 1997: 41)

At the heart of this idea of leisure is an imbroglio so complex and in many other respects so simple that it does not transfer so easily into words. However, a critical observation lies at the heart of Aristotle's thesis: 'we mistake leisure for idleness, and work for creativity. Of course, work may be creative. But only when informed by leisure. Work is the means of life; leisure the end' (Scruton, 1998: xii). Such an understanding of leisure, we might respond, is no longer suitable for explaining modern realties: on the one hand it is utopian (a description of leisure, rather than leisure in the actual making) and on the other it evokes the kind of sanguinity that our more cynical modern age has forgotten. However, it is important to be aware of the understanding of leisure through the classical intellectual tradition, because not only does it identify two further family concepts – as we will see in Chapter 2 pleasure and happiness are affecting concepts from which we can still learn a great deal – that might help us to grasp the modern sense of leisure, but it also helps to explain why leisure is a part of our *doxa* (the knowledge we think with but not about).

ETYMOLOGICAL DEFINITIONS OF LEISURE

Another way in which we might try to understand modern leisure is by exploring the etymology of the word. In *The Sage Dictionary of Leisure Studies* (2009), I suggest that there are three distinct but not unrelated etymological sources of modern understandings of leisure. There is the more obvious old French term *leisir*, itself derived from the Latin root *licēre*. *Licēre* is especially interesting because in its duality it reveals that the idea of leisure abounds with ambivalence: on the one hand it relates to freedom but on the other it is also a term, which as its root suggests, that signifies permission or licence. There is also a sense of ambivalence reflected in the distinction between the two other etymological sources, both of which are less noticeably related to the modern word. The first of these is the term *ōtiōsus* meaning 'leisured'. *Ōtiōsus* is a transfiguration of the older Latin term *ōtium* which until the eighteenth century simply means leisure. As we will see in Chapter 3, from this historical juncture, however, *ōtium* and its derivatives become synonymous with leisure time which may or may not be used for self-improvement.

The other etymological source is the Greek term *skholē*, which at its most basic level of understanding simply means to be free from obligation. As we saw from Bourdieu's (1999) definition in the introduction, however, this idea is also another word for the spade work needed to fire what the Canadian cultural critic Northrop Frye (1963) calls the 'educated imagination', which, freed from the necessities of day-to-day existence, allows unbridled and original ideas to prosper, giving us a perspective on reality that we don't get in any other way. What this suggests is that Bourdieu's definition only just begins to account for the scope and the significance of the idea of *skholē*, which as this second reading from Aristotle in the quotation below tells us, doesn't just train the mind, to paraphrase Frye, but also affects our whole social and moral development.

> Aristotle said that the aim of education is to equip us to make noble use of our leisure: and this fine sentiment implies that leisure is properly an opportunity to enjoy what makes us flourish: to pursue the arts, to reflect, to deepen understanding, to further friendships, and to pursue excellence. If work is concerned with securing life's necessities, leisure is concerned with cultivating its amenities.
>
> (Grayling, 2000)

It is important to note that s*kholē* was also considered by the Greeks to be an ideal state guided by the appreciation of moderation. Roger Scruton (2009) offers a precise account of this facility in his discussion of sex. What might be said about drinking or smoking applies equally to sex Scruton suggests: it is necessary to 'acquire the right habit – in other words, to school oneself' into having the right amount of sex, on the right occasions and for the right length of time. With an echo to Foucault (1979), who brings to our attention the fact that in classical Greek society adult men with wives and partners would on occasions have sex with their male apprentices, and this was considered to be normal, Scruton reasons that the Greeks defined the problem of sex as to want to have sex all the time, to want to have sex on the wrong occasions and for the wrong length of time. This makes for self-caricature and is to act like a clown; and to be a clown is to live an entertaining, though limited, life. What this shows is that the Greeks, in their rebuke to the *ótiose* life (any kind of sloth), considered every kind of leisure to be a serious business – both a privileged and studious occupation – which suggests that it also needs to be understood as a restrictive economy of pleasure.

As Thomas (2009: 78) points out, Greek elites also promoted the idea that life would be better if we had no work at all: 'the best life was one of leisure: not idleness, of course, but virtuous activity of mind and body, involving no manual labour and unconstrained by the need to earn a living'. As this observation suggests, if seriousness was a vital aspect of *skholē* what it also contained was the tacit acknowledgement of an affiliation between leisure and work; and not only that, but if leisure might be a serious, spiritual activity that bears all that is virtuous about humankind's non-obligated endeavours, it is only the preserve of a small minority possessing the necessary education and economic freedom from having to earn a living.

From its very origins in Greek thought, then, we can see that there are a number of connections between leisure and work. Clearly the Greeks thought that work was an overrated virtue and that life would be better were people not to work at all. However, as Thomas suggests, for the Greeks, leisure was not really understood through its oppositional relationship to work, but in opposition to the sin of idleness. It is quite an historical jump to move from discussing leisure in the classical Greek world to the beginning of modernity in England. But here too there is a similar view about idleness, which emerges in the post-Reformation period. In Chapter 3, I shall pursue this connection by examining closely the specific way in which Christianity followed in the footsteps of the classical Greek world, by developing its own special reading of the Bible which understood that those 'who followed the path of desires, pleasures, emotions and any feelings not unconditionally controlled by spiritually, were regarded not just as inferior men, but as sinners' (Heller, 2009: 2). For the moment, however, we need to look in more detail at the important relationship between leisure and work.

LEISURE AND WORK

This seemingly indelible relationship has undergone considerable debate in leisure studies, to the extent that it is now readily understood as a conceptual couplet (Blackshaw and Crawford, 2009). Where was once a tendency to treat the relationship between leisure and work in over-simplistic terms, with the former understood as a residual category of, or an oppositional response to, the latter (Lundberg *et al.*, 1934). That is, leisure is something that people do on an evening or at the weekend when they are not at work or it symbolizes an act of resistance to people's dissatisfaction with work. In this view, leisure is seen as something that is 'ostensibly private, individual and free as opposed to work which is public, social and regulated' (Slater, 1998: 396).

As I explain in *The Dictionary of Leisure Studies* (2009), writing in the 1970s and early 1980s, Parker (1976; 1983) suggested that, although work takes up only a portion of people's lives, their leisure activities are undoubtedly conditioned by the various factors associated with the ways they work. People who work together are not only assembled in the same time and space, but are also required to focus their collective attention on a common objective or activity, which means that they also share a common experience of work, whether it is positive, negative or neutral. Consequently, Parker concluded that, for most people, their leisure is shaped by how they react to work and its authority predominates over other influences, such as class and gender (Clarke and Critcher, 1985). What this suggests is that leisure cannot simply be understood as reflecting a particular form of work; it is necessary to understand the specific nature and conditions of that work experience, which are pervasive.

Parker's research led him to conclude that the relationship between work and leisure tends to fall into three categories: the opposition pattern (e.g. those who are in physically hard and dangerous occupations often try to escape from hardships of work through drinking and gambling with work-mates), the neutrality pattern (repetitive or routine work has a tendency to lead to apathy and indifference in the work place and this is reflected in people's leisure activities which tend to be monotonous and passive) and the extension pattern (those who have high levels of personal commitment to their work and get a good deal of job satisfaction are more likely to extend work related social networks and activities into their leisure time).

While such research was important to understanding how inextricably intertwined the relationship between leisure and work is in modern societies and how any adequate theory of leisure must take work into account, it has been criticized on a number of counts (Blackshaw and Crawford, 2009). First, there are simply too many exceptions to the work-leisure couplet, the most conspicuous being the non-employed, such as the elderly, and those people not in paid work, such as the unemployed and carers (especially many women), whose experiences of leisure are often fragmented and unpredictable. This leads to a second problem with the work-leisure couplet, that is that it marginalizes the extent to which the home is for many women a place of work (e.g. domestic labour, home-working) – albeit one that is not recognized by society as such. Third, the work-leisure couplet focuses its attention much less on what people do in their leisure time and more on leisure as a residual category of work; and to this extent it offers an overly functionalist understanding of leisure. Indeed, contrary to Parker (1976; 1983), and as we will see in the discussion of leisure and freedom below, many people today would argue that it is their leisure that is utterly bound up with who they are, and their identities, not their work.

This last point notwithstanding, it has been compellingly argued by a number of scholars that in a work-based society dominated by capitalist accumulation leisure itself has become functionalist in the sense that it is deeply commodified and used to accomplish the need to sell more consumer goods. Slater (1998: 401) asserts that it in this way leisure ends up being 'ideologically sold to us as a sphere of freedom from work, from public responsibilities and obligations ... it is part of a deal that in exchange for all this "freedom" and "pleasure" – it secures docile workers and citizens'. As we will see in Chapter 4, more recently developed theoretical approaches suggest that there has been a relaxing of the societal hold that the work ethic once had and it has been supplanted by an aesthetic of consumerism (Bauman, 1998). Rutherford (2007: 46) supports this view, arguing that religious anxiety about 'How can I be good?' has by now turned into the secular 'How can I be happy?'

Moreover, there is increasing evidence to suggest that with the consolidation of what have been called post-Fordist working practices, whereby mass, centralized industrial (Fordist) working practices give way to more flexible, decentralized forms of the labour process, work and leisure have once again become de-differentiated (Rojek, 2010). Poder's (2007) research, for example, suggests that it is increasingly the case that people do not so much value their leisure time over work, but think of work in similar ways to what they think and feel about consuming. That is, the point of being in work is not just about having a job: it should be exciting, stimulating and challenging and make us happy. One of the upshots of this is that work (like leisure) has developed an aesthetical significance, which not only means that it increasingly individualizes our experiences of employment so that they are not easily shared with others, but also therefore makes shared responses to discontent in the workplace more unlikely.

Work, unemployment and leisure

No discussion of the relationship between leisure and work can avoid the issue of unemployment. If work is the thing that gives you your sense of who you are or it simply makes you happy, or it provides the economic means for achieving these sorts of things in your leisure, what happens if you lose your job? As I have argued elsewhere, unemployment, otherwise known as the involuntary or voluntary lack of paid work, has considerable implications for people's lives generally and their leisure opportunities specifically (Blackshaw and Crawford, 2009). Unemployment is a complex process but it can nonetheless be divided into a number of sub-categories: *frictional* unemployment which arises as a result of movement in the job market as people move from one job to another; *seasonal* unemployment such as it occurs in the leisure and tourism industries as a result of changes in supply and demand; *cyclical* unemployment caused by the swinging pendulums that are the business and trade cycles; and *structural* unemployment, where significant changes in the global economy lead to large numbers of people losing their jobs.

On the face of it the major trend in Western economies since the mid-1960s has seen employment in services grow and employment in manufacturing decline. However, this trend masks the fact that the decline in manufacturing has also been accompanied by technological changes and changes in production associated with the substitution of post-Fordist work practices for Fordist work practices (see Harvey, 1989) and the global restructuring of industrial labour on neo-liberal lines, two processes which have increased productivity while dispensing with the need for unskilled and semi-skilled workers, and sometimes even highly skilled workers. The upshot of these changes is that compared with the period of relative full employment, which occurred in the late-1950s and 1960s, unemployment rates in Western countries have increased dramatically and long term unemployment is by now a persistent problem. It should also be noted that unemployment is on the whole a *selective* process: different *social groups* experience different levels of unemployment; for example, it tends to be higher for women, ethnic minority groups and young people, and job losses tend to be regional, and as a result are experienced as *geographically* uneven.

In her pioneering book *Leisure and Unemployment* Glyptis (1989: 159) observes that 'work and leisure are not just a conceptual couplet, twinned for the convenience of testing theories. They are experienced as a couplet, the one deriving meaning from the other.' Indeed, the loss of work through unemployment has some profound implications for patterns of participation in leisure activities as well as for individuals and society more generally. When individuals become unemployed they lose the income, social networks, identity, status and self-esteem which are obtained through work. If their unemployment is long term the incessant search for work and the stigma associated with welfare dependence are likely to lead to the development of shame and the sense of personal failing. One of the foremost consequences of long term unemployment is social isolation, with the loss of friendships garnered through work; this situation is exacerbated because individuals have little disposable income to spend on by now taken-for-granted leisure activities, such as going to the cinema, eating out and having a drink at the local pub. In a nutshell, unemployment means more 'free time' for individuals with little money, confidence or inclination to enjoy it.

What should not be overlooked, however, is that unemployment can provide an unprecedented opportunity to get involved in new leisure activities and leisure education, which can in turn lead to hitherto unimagined experiences and even offer new openings in the job market. Nevertheless this view is highly contested, not least because work remains the major source of value in society.

The consequences of unemployment for society are less obvious but equally significant for leisure participation. Evidence shows that in societies where high levels of unemployment persist, the likelihood is that there will emerge more discipline in the workplace, leading to increased working hours and more uncertainty amongst the employed. As Kane (2006) argues, in such a scenario work tends to make individuals less happy, unhealthy and confused, at the same time as dissolving the dignity and respect it affords them in conditions of full employment. It is the unemployed themselves who bear the brunt of high unemployment, however, with society seeing rising levels of poverty, homelessness and family breakdown and concomitant problems such as mental illness, increased levels of crime, violence, alcoholism, drug misuse and suicide. Evidence also shows that another significant societal trend that emerges in such circumstances is more racism as those most affected by unemployment lay the blame for their circumstances on ethnic minority and immigrant groups.

What the forgoing discussion suggests is that not only are the symptoms and pain of unemployment both *private* and concealed within people's homes and *public* and revealed in the way that a society constitutes and imagines itself, but they also have massive implications for how people experience leisure both individually and collectively.

LEISURE AS FREEDOM

Whereas leisure studies scholars such as Parker restrict their discussions about leisure primarily to the ways in which it is shaped by work, Ken Roberts extends the boundaries of discussion a little more to argue that leisure is basically '*spare* or *free time* in which we can please ourselves; the part of life that remains when we have fulfilled our duties' (1981: 9–10). The changed emphasis on free time rather than work fails, however, to elide the fundamental sense that leisure is still seen as a residual category of experience. It is in this sense that Roberts' definition differs from that of Raymond Williams who argues that 'the real dividing line between the things we call work and the things we call leisure is that in leisure, however active we may be, we make our own choices and our own decisions; we feel for the time being that our life is our own' (1961; cited in Veal, 1992). What Williams' interpretation suggests is that the real key to understanding leisure is not work or residual time when we have fulfilled the rest of our obligations, but freedom.

It is not difficult to understand why the notion of freedom is central to the vocabulary of leisure. After all, leisure as freedom is embodied with a dialectic which, to use Giddens' (1984) apt expression, is reflective of the double hermeneutic that is the measure of the idea as it is used on the one hand by men and women in their day-to-day lives (even if, as it was pointed out in the introduction, most of the time they don't actually call it leisure), and on the other as it is used by sociologists and other social scientists. This is what leads Roberts (1978: 3) to deduce that the idea of leisure 'as relatively freely undertaken nonwork activity is broadly consistent with everyday use of the term, and can also be a penetrating sociological formula'.

The central idea of linking nonwork activity with freedom is located in definitions of leisure as 'free-time' activity, for which some leisure studies scholars tend to offer the best understandings of modern leisure available (Shivers and deLisle, 1997). However, to say that leisure is simply free time, that is, an occasion, opportunity or period free from other obligations, when an individual is able to organize his or her own time in whatever ways he or she sees appropriate, tells us nothing about the content and quality of the leisure experienced. Such a definition also ignores the fact that time free to make deliberative choices about what to do with one's free time is always accompanied by the implication that the individual's ability to enjoy his or her free time has been, or is potentially, open to restraint or constraint. Such a definition, if it is useful for identifying in broad terms the quantity of time available for leisure, and how time is distributed among different social and cultural groups, also ignores, or at least marginalizes, how that free time has been created. For example, has the individual in question lost his or her job? Is he or she simply filling in time? Has he or she been forcibly retired? And so on. It is for these reasons that the notion of 'free time' for leisureliness, like Bertrand Russell's dictum that liberty is 'the absence of obstacles to the realization of desire', is inadequate.

Leisure as flow

Numerous other scholars have also suggested that leisure is not necessarily proscribed by the demands of work, but is instead often less clearly defined in people's actual day-to-day lives. In Dumazedier's (1974: 133) thesis, for example, leisure is 'activity – apart from the obligations of work, family, and society – to which the individual turns at will, for either relaxation, diversion, or broadening his knowledge and his spontaneous social participation, the free exercise of his creative capacity'. In this way we might say that leisure is inspiring despite its ordinariness since, although it is something that seems tacit, it nonetheless engrosses the foreground of our productive energies, permeating some of our fundamental attitudes to aspiration, enthralment and exhilaration. Cushman and Laidler (cited in Veal, 1992), in an extension of this thought, argue that leisure is first and foremost

> a state of being, an attitude of mind or a quality of experience ... It is distinguished *by* the individual's perceived freedom to act and distinguished *from* conditions imposed by necessity ... It is assumed to be pleasurable and, although it may appeal because of certain anticipated benefits, it is intrinsically motivated: it is an end in itself and valuable for its own sake.

Csikszentmihalyi (1974) is not a leisure scholar per se, but his work is important as it is the definitive illustration of leisure of the kind that is that characterized by 'flow', or the existential experience of total involvement in leisure activities, freely chosen, which are self-rewarding and contain an uncertainty of outcome that allows for individual creativity. The idea is that leisure allows individuals to enter a world of flow or a stream of super-consciousness – a relationship with time, space and experience that is far removed from everyday experience. As well as being current, flow is also open to possibility, allowing creativity to move through individuals who are at one with both the process and the content of the leisure activity in question. To this extent, flow is related to other humanistic psychological motivational concepts, such as the need for self-actualization associated with the work of Abraham Maslow (e.g. 1968) and Carl Rogers (e.g. 1961) which has been used to explore opportunities for human innovation and creativeness.

In developing his ideas, Csikszentmihalyi argues that the level of leisure activities should be matched to individual skill. Tennis is the game he usually uses to illustrate how certain leisure activities promote flow and to demonstrate how it is possible to measure the value of flow to individuals. A game of tennis, he argues, is only enjoyable when two players are evenly matched, which suggests that uncertainty is a precondition of optimal flow and that satisfaction occurs at the border line between boredom and anxiety, when the challenges of the contest are precisely balanced with each player's individual ability to act. Rojek adds to this psychological understanding a sociological dimension which takes account of the quickening and slowing down of flow through the concepts of 'fast' and 'slow' leisure. As Rojek demonstrates, these enable us to account for the ways in which 'flow alters the quantitative and intensity of our relationships with others, and, through this, the [ways in which the] character of leisure is altered' (2000: 22).

According to Csikszentmihalyi flow activities have as their prime purpose the pursuit of pleasure and happiness. Consequently individuals undergoing deep flow will often find the leisure activity so totally engrossing that not only does a transmogrification of time occur, but they can also lose self-consciousness. This is described as the autotelic experience of deep flow wherein engagement in a particular leisure activity ostensibly leads to individual transcendence. Csikszentmihalyi is also keen to stress that such experiences do not always need to give immediate gratification, noting that the journey to optimal or deep flow does not always feel pleasurable at the time (as in the case of a physically and mentally challenging sport or adventure activity), but can be achieved later, through reflection.

Here the vital insight is that in modern societies leisure is often the emotional centre of people's lives. For those individuals who seek freedom through deep flow, the real focus of their lives is not work (or anything else) but leisure. The psychologist of leisure John Neulinger (1974) concludes that the only proper definition of leisure is this subjective one, because not only does it offer the experience of a unique state of being, but it is also entered into voluntarily and in this way is motivating of its own merit. To illustrate this conception let us consider Joyce Carol Oates' (2008) review of Annie Proulx's portrait of wilderness travel in her novel *Fine Just the Way It Is*. In this book Proulx describes a young couple, Caitlin and Marc, whose lives are 'suffused with euphoria' for wilderness travel and its difficult and solitary travails:

> As many days and weeks as they could manage they spent hiking the Big Horns, the Wind Rivers, exploring old logging roads, digging around ancient mining claims. Marc had a hundred plans. He wanted to canoe the Boundary Waters, to kayak down the Labrador coast, to fish in Peru. They snowboarded the Wasatch, followed wolf packs in Yellowstone's backcountry. They spent long weekends in Utah's Canyonlands, in Wyoming's Red Desert Haystacks looking for fossils. The rough country was their emotional center.
>
> (quoted in Oates, 2008)

What is being suggested here is that leisure presents, to Caitlin and Marc, and other women and men like them, not only a means of connecting with nature but the possibility of the essential meaning of life itself, and, more than that, a kind of transcendence that gives them a sense of authenticity that is spiritual. It is as if their leisure makes them, and not them their leisure. Terry Eagleton (2007) argues that such self-realization is achieved through precisely this loss of the self in leisure (in Eagleton's own example it is being part of a jazz band), and that this might just provide us with the meaning of life. The appeal of leisure here is on the one hand its uncertainty, and the freedom that that uncertainty brings, that constitutes its allure, and on the other, a sense of community with a common purpose as well as a shared understanding of a moral code. However, what Eagleton perhaps overlooks is that, in common with other liminal experiences (we will look at this concept in Chapter 2), what is the most powerful dimension of any flow experience is its solitariness; the way it emphasizes, not so much a sense of coming together, but the individual's existential freedom from others.

While Csikszentmihalyi's particular understanding of self-realization through flow is undoubtedly helpful to understanding of the restorative emotional effects of leisure, as well as the ways in which it has the capacity to reveal to individuals existential insights into the way that they live their lives, it is for some critics ultimately too psychologistic (Rojek, 2000), in the sense that its understanding of freedom is an empty concept since it does not ask the questions, 'freedom from what? and, freedom from whom?' (Rojek, 2010: 181). What this suggests is that seeing leisure as flow activity in terms of absolute human freedom is naïve.

LEISURE AS UNFREEDOM

It would appear from the psychological perspective discussed above that the true terrain of leisure is the interior of the human mind, a way of seeing, an outlook turned on the world rather than simply reflecting it. And that it is this outlook, from the inside out, that counts when we try to understand leisure. What this perspective fails to take sufficiently into account, however, is that freedom is a duality: 'the difference between action dependent on the will of others and action dependent on one's own will' (Bauman, 1988: 9). It is in this social relation that we also find the ambivalence of leisure: on the one hand it is an idea that always implies freedom but on the other it is also one that always signifies constraint. Structuralist critics of this psychological perspective have argued that although it would appear that we have freedom to choose our leisure, modern society actually denies us real choice. Rather than looking at freedom, these critics suggest, we should be concerned with trying to make sense of leisure by interpreting leisure practice independently of the experiences of those who experience it. A good recent example of this kind of interpretation is Dennis and Urry's (2009) study of the motor car. Their analysis suggests that car driving is not so much a leisure interest that presents the individual with more freedom, so much that the car itself is a major component of a system which gives the illusion of freedom while adhering its users into a dependence on highly dense traffic management, oil, and the means to pay for oil and causing untold ecological damage to the planet.

What Dennis and Urry (2009) are suggesting here is that we engage with leisure activities such as motor car driving ideologically with false consciousness, or what might be described as action without awareness or cognizant knowledge. This idea is taken to be one of the fundamental premises of Marxism. False consciousness is understood in Marxist terms not as a natural event, nor is it the creation of our own imaginations, but rather it is something imposed upon us from above through the 'dominant ideology'. In this view social relations embody a struggle of conflicting class interests. However, this struggle is largely invisible and everyone tends to assume that how things appear to be is how they actually and inevitably are – this is what neo-Marxist sociologists call hegemony. In our example, the dominant ideology 'naturalizes' the idea that car driving is the ultimate route to freedom in modern societies and environmental degradation and resource depletion are not really important issues.

The strength of this type of critique is that it demonstrates that leisure is actually difficult to define as freedom in a straightforward way. And not only that, and more importantly, that as a central idea of social science it is also indistinguishable from social and economic inequality, power and social control, and consumer capitalism. To use an expression coined by Max Weber, what is implied in Dennis and Urry's account is that modernity is a 'disenchanted' world which is characterized by a deficit of meaning and a loss of individual autonomy and leisure as freedom is impossible. If we want to find the real meaning and purpose of leisure, as well as what the constraints to its actualization are, we must uncover the falsehoods underpinning the dominant ideology which guides thinking and action in the modern world. What this suggests is that structuralist critics believe that modern society has had and continues to have a long-standing and steady negative relationship with leisure.

THE LIMITS OF STRUCTURALIST UNDERSTANDINGS OF LEISURE AS FREEDOM

A somewhat different position is taken by Bauman and Žižek. They argue that the world we inhabit today is one 'emancipated from false consciousness' (Bauman, 1992: 188). Bauman, in common with those looking at leisure from a structuralist perspective, recognizes that capitalism sees us as consumers (in our example consumers of oil) and wants nothing more from us than our capacity 'to stay in the game and have enough tokens left on the table to go on playing' (Bauman, 2004: 52). However, he also argues that we are in effect forced to forge a sense of identity in a world less relentlessly defined by class ideology and more by consumerism. Bauman also understands, in common with Žižek (1989), that the contingent worlds that constitute the modern world today operate as a matter of *action in spite of knowledge:* individuals in their roles as consumers are not so much brainwashed by ideology as lacking the appetite for the class struggle – ideologies are relegated to the background, while a hegemonic embracement of capitalism discloses a sense of what is really at stake: a consumer existence versus an authentic life.

In this sense Bauman's sociology captures the irony that if for the majority of men and women the beginning of the modern era was a time when freedom was seen as an astonishing but largely unachievable hope, today we appear to be prepared to surrender our hard fought freedoms to the vast decentred power-knowledge of consumer capitalism, which we happily allow to not so much regulate, as *deregulate* our lives. In relation to our topic, what this means is that leisure has by and large been turned into consuming and most of us into ubiquitous sale shoppers too heavily weighed down by all the delightful purchases we have been making to devote any of our time to what leisure really has to offer us. And regardless of this knowledgability, we are even prepared to embrace the burgeoning debt culture that accompanies this shop-until-you-drop performance.

In the event, Marxists and other more contemporary adherents of 'dominant ideological' explanations, such as Habermas (1976), who argue that leisure, rather than being an alternative to work has merely become a part of the rationalization of labour, are confronted with the quandary of revealing 'structures of domination when no one is dominating, nothing is being dominated, and no ground exists for a principle of liberation from domination' (Poster, 1994). What this suggests is that it is the configuration of economic arrangements associated with consumer capitalism which is of far greater importance for explaining patterns of social control today. To put it another way, social control (like most leisure) in liberal democracies has by and large been commodified and privatized. The comfortable majority no longer live in the shadow of tyranny of the state; instead they create their own turmoil, or in Baudrillard's (1998) terminology, their own paroxysm, driven by market forces that they have no authority over, but at the same time have no final authority over them. The turmoil is barely noticeable – publicly at least – it is simply how people live and how they leisure. As Bauman puts it, it is as if 'we have been trained to stop worrying about things which stay stubbornly beyond our power ... and to concentrate our attention and energy instead on the tasks within our (individual) reach, competence and capacity for consumption (2004: 74).

Fantasy leisure

The other key factor that structural theories of leisure fail sufficiently to take into account is that leisure is a landmark of our fantasy behaviour. We all know what fantasy leisure is. It involves the pleasure and enjoyment we get from the creativity of the human imagination, which allows us to make our own lives extraordinary. As Harris (2005) points out, fantasy leisure is directed and controlled by the same motives and interests that drive all other leisure activities – the pursuit of pleasure. This is a particular kind of pleasure which arises from treating the world out there as if it is at the same time separate and 'other', but also customary and clearly recognizable. Harris also suggests that it is through making this distinction that we can make sure that our fantasies combine the allure of the unexpected with just the right amount of challenge.

The idea of fantasy leisure is explored to good effect by Andrew O'Hagan (2009) in his essay *Car of One's Own*. O'Hagan makes many of the same critical points that Dennis and Urry make about the function of cars in modern societies, but where he departs from them is in the way he discloses the existential freedom he gets from driving. 'The first long drive I took after passing my test', he writes, 'was a kind of baptism':

> I put down the windows and let all life's unreasonable demarcations fly behind the car, enjoying the illusion that I now had a friend who cared for my freedom ... I could easily say I loved my car – I missed it when I went to bed at night. On that first long drive from London to Wales and thence to Inverness – which took 14 hours – I believe I discovered my autonomy. As with all illusions, I didn't care that others found the enchantment funny: the feeling was new, and its newness is something that millions of people express rarely but understand fully. In American fiction, a great number of epiphanies – especially male epiphanies – occur while the protagonist is alone and driving his car. There are reasons for that. One may not have a direction but one has a means of getting there. One may not be in control of life but one can progress in a straight line. When your youth is over and definitions become fixed, even if they are wrong, it might turn out that the arrival of a car suddenly feels like the commuting of a sentence. It may seem to give you back your existential mojo. That is the beauty of learning to drive late and learning to drive often: it gives you a sense that life turned out to be freer than it was in your childhood, that time agrees with you, that your own sensitivities found their domain in the end, and that deep in the shell of your inexpensive car you came to know your subjectivity. Of course, one

may find these things in the marriage bed or in a gentleman's club, but those places have rules and your car is your own bed, your own club. Music? Yes. Tears? Yes. Singing? Yes. Stopping under the stars? OK, if you must. And here is Tintern Abbey. And there is Hadrian's Wall. And should I stop in Glasgow for a drink? If you read the novels of Joan Didion, you will see there can come a time in anybody's life, women's as much as men's, when they climb into their car and feel that they are driving away from an entire kingdom of dependency.

What this quotation suggests is we should not be content with structural interpretations of leisure, because they fail to take fully into account the different ways in which we might understand freedom. Indeed, understanding how freedom works is much more complex than we might think, as the French philosopher Jean-Paul Sartre (for whom the fundamental fact of the human condition is freedom of choice) explains, since it is often the case that freedom is not destroyed by structural constraints, but is in fact made more real by them. What Sartre is offering here is an existential understanding of freedom which as well as arguing that human beings are 'not free to cease being free', suggests we must always take into account the common features of the situations which individuals find themselves in. So, for example, when a nation is invaded and occupied by a foreign power, Sartre argues, as in the case of the German occupation of France in the Second World War, individuals often find in this kind of situation a way to be free. In other words, we are never freer than when we are constrained.

What structuralist accounts also tend to overlook is that leisure can paradoxically be a demonstration of the desire *for* unfreedom or constraint. Another existential philosopher Albert Camus famously argued that it is servitude that is actually the real passion of the modern age. A good example of leisure with which to explore these kinds of ideas is the sexual practice of sadomasochism. Referred to colloquially as S/M or S&M, sadomasochism, as its nomenclature suggests, is a leisure activity that combines sadist and masochist sexual practices, and often with bondage: on the sadism side is the intense pleasure of inflicting pain or humiliation on another who is constrained in some way (e.g. tied up or handcuffed); and on the masochism side the intense pleasure gained through receiving pain and/or being humiliated whilst being constrained. Just as sadist activities provide some individuals with sexual gratification because they are free, so masochist activities provide others with sexual gratification because they are unfree. For Foucault, S/M at the moment of its realization, is everything, since it incorporates new pleasures, such pleasures that pleasure is perhaps not a word capable of identifying with the kind of pleasure the pleasure that it brings. In other words, S/M provides its participants with the highest of the high, or what Edmund Burke (1729–97) called the sublime, which finds its source in anything capable of exciting extremes of pleasure and pain. As Foucault puts it in his own inimitable way:

> The idea of S/M is related to deep violence, that S/M practice is a way of liberating that violence, this aggression, is stupid. We all know very well that what all these people are doing is not aggressive; they are inventing new possibilities of pleasure with strange parts of their body – through the eroticisation of the body. I think it is a kind of creation, a creative enterprise, which has as one of its main features what I call the desexualisation of pleasure ... The possibility of using our bodies as a possible source of very numerous pleasures is something that is important.
>
> (Foucault quoted in Robinson, 2003: 137)

Foucault would argue, contrary to Sartre, that the kind of freedom S/M offers resides within the discourse within which it is framed, rather than in the mind of the beholder: the shift from the truth about social reality to discursive formations with an emphasis on contingency *and* the rejection of the notion of the centred subject with clear intent and agency. What this suggests is that not only is it the human imagination that is crucial to understanding leisure as freedom (and unfreedom), but that the cultural context in which it takes place as well as the contingencies of circumstance also matters. The other key point to make is that there are of course some men and women who are attracted to S/M simply because they want risk, mess and transgression, but there are others who only want it with the risk and messiness cleaned up and the transgression staged: in other words, leisure that is mimetic and just a bit of fun. This is what Blackshaw and Crabbe (2004) call 'consumptive deviance'.

Either way, it is in their leisure that a lot of men and women live dangerously (or dangerously only vicariously), where they can make believe all the things that they cannot (or refuse) to do in their 'real' lives. In other words, it is in our leisure where we can address the limits of the contingency of our individual place in the world by transcending it; we may never be able to completely lose our social class, gender or ethnic identities, but this does not stop us trying. Seen in this way it is in our leisure pursuits that we seek and can reconcile a desperate wish for pleasure (and pain) with an intractable feeling of a sort of non-existence. This is nothing new, as Matt Houlbrook (2005) demonstrates in his perceptive historical study of queer London in the first half of the twentieth century, a lively working-class street life of same sex sexual relations co-existing with 'normal' heterosexual life. As Houlbrook shows, to borrow an expression from Richard Hornsey (2006), just as some 'heterosexual' men enjoyed the occasional bit of 'bum fun' with their 'homosexual' counterparts, others were not averse to selling their bums for cash or the excitement of what Adam Philips calls the 'the unlived life that seems the only life worth living' (2003: 9).

As Freud would have put it, these kinds of leisure activities provide a direct challenge to the assumed authority of the 'reality principle' by the 'pleasure principle'. For Freud (1950) the 'pleasure principle' is a tendency inherent in the unconscious of all individuals and involves their 'wishes' to seek their own satisfactions regardless of all other considerations. In early modern societies the suppression of these 'wishes' operated through the 'reality principle'. But the price of the triumph of the 'reality principle' was the temporary suspension of the 'pleasure principle', which had to be put off *ad infinitum*. In the event society reached a status quo of sorts by 'allowing' men and women to achieve the utmost possible expression of their desires with 'normalizing' conditions. Basically, shame was what maintained the 'reality principle', i.e. having a 'bit of bum fun' is unworthy of somebody 'normal'. That is individuals had to be sure they knew the differences between 'fantasy' and 'reality' in accord with the demands of the 'reality principle'. People were of course wont to take some risks in their leisure but this did not ultimately ever lead to the complete undermining of the overall moral order of society because, as Rojek (1995: 88) points out, with the 'reality principle' intact:

> rather than complete suspension of morality one finds the lifting of the curtain of morals followed by embarrassed or guilty returns to moral codes … And so the attempt to escape perishes because it depends upon the very conventions that make everyday life possible. By searching for the total sexual encounter, the orgy of freedom and self-expression, the unbridled carnivalesque and the other 'real' experiences which lie beyond civil society, we collide with the antinomies of our desire.

What this tells us then is that freedom (and unfreedom) in leisure is not only contingent but also temporal. Here we also see that leisure has the important societal function of maintaining society's moral universe. In Foucault's universe, however, there perhaps lies another understanding of leisure. He came to believe that of consenting men in 1970s California S/M could be the basis of the invention of a new sexuality from nowhere. In other words, sex is neither an unchanging historical constant nor a primordial drive fighting free of the reality principle, but something culture makes and unmakes (Jones, 2007). What this suggests for our study is that trying to understand leisure 'as a bounded category of practice and experience', formed in an idiom which places so much emphasis on the value of functionality is insufficient to understanding the relationship between freedom and leisure, and this needs to be subsumed into the subject of culture (Rojek, 1995). We will return to this topic in Chapter 5. It is to a consideration of some further uses of leisure that we next turn.

CONCLUSION

This chapter has looked at the idea of leisure, focusing in particular on etymological definitions, the relationship between leisure and work and the debate about whether or not leisure is another expression of freedom.

We saw that:

- the idea of leisure abounds with ambivalence: on the one hand it suggests freedom but on the other it is also a term that signifies restraint, moderation, permission, licence, constraint and social control;
- in all definitions of leisure there appears to be some connection to work and the relationship between these two concepts is complicated;
- work is the economic means for achieving the things that we aspire, to in our leisure and without work our leisure is likely to be circumscribed, but not necessarily so;
- leisure can be defined as free time but this tells us little about how we experience it;
- psychological theories, such as flow, tell us a great deal about the relationship between leisure and self-discovery;
- freedom is *always* a social relation and leisure as freedom is an empty concept if it does not recognize this;

- structuralist theories seek to understand the meaning of leisure by interpreting leisure practice independently of the experiences of those who experience it;
- structural theories stress the importance of 'dominant ideologies' and 'hegemony' in socially controlling us and constraining our opportunities for leisure;
- critics of structural approaches argue that consumerism is of far greater importance for explaining patterns of social control today;
- we need to understand not just how we choose our leisure, but also how it chooses us; this tells us that how we *experience* leisure is very important;
- leisure is a landmark of our fantasy behaviour;
- freedom is not necessarily destroyed by structural constraints, but can in fact be made more real by them;
- unfreedom is an important aspect of some people's leisure;
- the situation or the context in which leisure is experienced is very important.

2

THE USES OF LEISURE: THREE PERSPECTIVES

In the last chapter, we started an intellectual journey that showed us that if the study of leisure seems at first glance like a single world-wide effort, it is really a progression of rivalries. To paraphrase and extend what Harvie Ferguson (2009: 10) recently said about *doing sociology*, we also took the first step in the process of reflecting on the variety and ambiguity of actual human experience; not with the aim of tidying-up the confusion emanating from these rivalries, eliminating their contradictions and setting out what leisure *should* mean, but trying to grasp and understand that complexity as part of the larger task of understanding the world itself, which as Northrop Frye (1963) says, 'never speaks unless we take the time to listen in leisure'. Now that we have a working definition of leisure, we need to outline the key leisure concepts, which suggests to me that we are about to take the next step on an intellectual journey, where we will not only learn a bit more about the larger task of understanding the world itself, but we might also begin to realize what it means to make our own free and liberated relation to the variety and ambiguity of actual human experience, which is desirable and rewarding in and for itself as a means towards our own personal fulfilment, but also dignity for the self and others.

If so short a book as this is to be of use to those wanting to learn about both the general and the particular aspects of the study of leisure, it will be necessary to be selective in our choice of leisure concepts. To this end I shall make an effort to characterize the contemporary nature of leisure studies in general, with examples drawn from theoretical developments and research in the field. But what to include? As I argued in the introduction, some concepts, especially those developed under the aegis of 1970s and 1980s leisure studies have been transformed by more recent societal changes and technological advances, in the process becoming grey areas of knowledge that have lost their former explanatory power. These will be included here in as far as they help us to try to get to grips with contemporary developments in the field. However, it is with leisure studies knowledge and issues of today that this book is primarily concerned. If some concepts traditionally associated with the subject field are not included it is because I thought that they no longer chime with the current needs of students and leisure scholars. Having said that, because this book is concerned with widening horizons, not narrowing them, what is identified and discussed in this chapter constitutes quite an extended family because, like the idea of leisure itself, the meaning of its key associated concepts – even the universal ones, such as play, which is one of the first to come under scrutiny in this chapter – is always fluid.

How can leisure be grasped conceptually? What, in other words, is distinctive of leisure? In seeking to answer such questions, I want to examine in turn three conceptual approaches, starting with the most familiar one, best exemplified in the work of Peter Borsay (2006), which not only identifies a combination of three essential elements of leisure: symbol, play and 'other', but also argues that if leisure has one inherent function quality, it is to provide a template upon which processes of societal continuity and change are acted out; continuing with a more controversial form of thinking in which it turns out that the 'leisure' under discussion is deviant or abnormal (Rojek, 2000), and which can involve violent and sadistic behaviour; and finally looking at leisure from the alternative perspective of it being, neither part of a tripartite tangle that it is ostensibly fixed once and for all, nor something abnormal, but a question of an uncomfortable coexistence: serious leisure and casual leisure. At each stage of this discussion I shall also offer my own critical interpretation of the three perspectives under scrutiny, which as the reader will see entails bringing to the table a whole host of other important leisure concepts.

THE ESSENTIAL ELEMENTS OF LEISURE

In *A History of Leisure* (2006), Peter Borsay approaches the topic of leisure in terms of the relation between symbolism, play and 'other'.

Echoing Rojek, Borsay's starting point is that the idea of leisure as freedom is unsatisfactory, since, as he asserts, although leisure studies theorists are well rehearsed in telling us what is meant by the idea of 'leisure as freedom from' (especially work), they are not very good at telling us what is meant by 'leisure as freedom to'. Borsay proffers that the pursuit of pleasure might be the answer, but rejects this on the basis that 'quite apart from the problem of accommodating recreations which embrace elements of pain and punishment, and there are surprisingly many of these, the notion remains too intangible to be satisfying' (p. 6).

Pleasure, desire and happiness

If we recall what Aristotle said about leisure at the beginning of Chapter 1, it would appear strange that anyone offering such a definitive conception of leisure would rule out any discussion of pleasure, especially since it is a quality of our individual subjectivity that is intimately tied up with our pursuit of happiness. From our own leisure experiences we all know the pleasure of anticipation going on a holiday brings, just as we have all experienced that kind of pleasure which makes us feel freshly grateful for being alive, for example, for the simple pleasure of reading or for the deviant delight of watching a favourite boxer drawing flesh and blood from the mouth of an opponent. What these kinds of observations suggest is that pleasure is something that belongs to the person who is experiencing it; as Harris (2005) points out, though, what they also tell us is that the presence of a pleasure might be one of *the* defining characteristics of leisure.

Drawing on the work of the French social theorist and semiologist, Roland Barthes, Harris identifies two kinds of pleasure that motivate our leisure: *plaisir* and *jouissance*. Making reference to our engagement with film and print media, he shows that the Barthesian understanding *plaisir* merely refers to the pleasure we gain from our passive engagement with novels and film, while *jouissance*, which hints at the idea of sexual pleasure, 'refers to something more intellectually ecstatic, the pleasures detectable in being able to recognize the effects of narrative on yourself, and, maybe, to begin to play with the novel or film, to weave your own narratives in and around it' (p. 197). What Barthes is referring to here is something like a confrontation with the sublime, which as Kant suggested, is the pleasurable fear we have to deal with when we cannot fully grasp or understand something that is overwhelming us, but which all the same prompts us to strive towards such understanding of it.

What this suggests is that the concept of desire is also important to understanding pleasure. At its most basic level of understanding this term is used to refer to things or persons we long or wish for. However, in the academic literature desire is understood as an eternal and recurring plane of consciousness that reflects the vitalism of human creativity and experience, described by the philosopher James Conant (cited in Williams, 1993) as the manifestation of 'our most profound confusions of soul', and by the film critic Peter Wollen (2007: 93) as something which is always competitive and in the final analysis 'implies the possibility of struggle and, inevitably, the risk of death, as occurs in wars'. To this extent leisure scholars must be capable of understanding desire, because doing so is also to understand how human beings think, speak, dream, imagine, live and die in the world.

Since the time of the Greeks, desire has been understood as something that is invariably in conflict with reason, which 'operates as a distinctive part of the soul'. According to Freudian analysts it is desire rather than reason that is the driving force behind human existence, even if it is not always acted upon. There is no doubt that people often live their lives sandwiched between named duty and unnamed desire – wishes that just must be made true. Yet if desire is always the possibility of wish fulfilment, this is often less than certain and expressions of desire tend to be intermittent and short-lived. What this Freudian understanding suggests is that there is something about desire that is irreconcilable with satisfaction.

It would also seem strange that *A History of Leisure* which, as we shall see in the next chapter, forcibly demonstrates that with the emergence of modern society, bourgeois values came to rest on the Puritan belief that pleasure was one thing and reality another, would begin and end without any discussion of Freud's (1950) key concepts of the 'pleasure principle' and the 'reality principle'. As we saw in the last chapter, these two concepts provided us with a useful way of trying to understand the dynamics of same-sex social relations in early twentieth century London (Houlbrook, 2005). The answer to this historical criticism also turns to a contemporary rejoinder: how do people use pleasure today? Building a sociological interpretation of this Freudian dichotomy, Bauman (2000a) has argued that the ideal bourgeois citizen of modernity in its 'solid', formative stage was cautious and apprehensive; was given to deferred gratification, considered the rainy days ahead, and was prepared to pay the price of present pleasures forgone, while the ideal bourgeois citizen of today is not averse to throwing caution to the wind and is on the contrary given to instant gratification, to putting off until further notice planning for future hardships, and unwilling to forgo present pleasures. In other words, men and women today find it impossible to censure and repress unconscious forces within them. Indeed, these days the pleasure of the fun we get from leisure is not the type of sin it used to be and the Puritanical notion that having fun is wrong has by now almost entirely disappeared and has been replaced by a civic duty to happiness.

Leisure as symbolism, play and 'other'

In marked contrast to the approach underpinning this book, which is concerned with the changing nature of the idea of leisure, Borsay argues that there is nonetheless a sense of continuity concerning that mode of human activity we know as 'leisure', which is offered by the three essential elements of symbolism, play and 'other'. As he points out, these three elements are not exclusive to leisure, but they are highly conspicuous in our leisure activities, are present in a specific combination, and our need for them in this combination is a historical constant. Borsay elaborates:

> By *symbol* is meant a notion of representation; a surrogate, image, or meta-phor for some other phenomenon. So, for example, the birds in a cockfight or mounts in a horse race could be said to represent their owners and those who bet on them, and piece of landscape to represent the nation. By *play* is meant something synthetic, unreal, and experimental; a self-contained activity without obvious consequence or significance, a mere game ... There is a fundamental social convention that leisure, however our experience might suggest otherwise, is not to be taken seriously; that as the spectator exits the cockpit, the theatre, the sports' stadium, the club and pub, he or she leaves the fantasy for the real world. The notion of a fantasy world is also implied by the idea of the *'other'*. This need not be confined to a specific location, though in the case of tourism and the holiday, place of vital significance, but can embrace any experience which is 'other' than that conceived of as normal.
>
> (2006: 6)

To appreciate leisure practice, Borsay's conceptualization suggests, we must recognize it is bound up with symbolism, myth and ritual, one that is explicitly part of a discourse about play and make believe, which appears at first sight as if it is separated off from the real world. The work of Huizinga is instructive here. For Huizinga (1955), play is older even than culture, since culture presumes human society, and animals did not have to wait for the evolution of humankind to teach them how to play. According to Huizinga, we can steadfastly assert from this observation alone that that humankind has added nothing to the essential basis of what constitutes play. In this view, play is the basis of human culture and in this regard it has a key functional role which stems from its non-seriousness and 'make-believe' status. There are a number of qualities that derive from this: play is free; play is self-contained – an end in itself; play is regulated or rule-bound; play is limited in time and space; play has an element of secrecy – an unknown know; and the outcome of play is uncertain (Haywood *et al.*, 1995). In Callois's (1961) thesis, Huizinga's theory of play as 'make-believe' is presented in more functional terms as an alternative to regulations in play which provides a means of recompense or sublimation for attitudes and activities that cannot find their expression in any other way.

In this sense the games that form the basis of play are best understood as a kind of cathartic release. At its most basic, catharsis means to purify or to clean. However, it is the psychoanalytical understanding of the concept that has generally been used in leisure studies. On the one hand, catharsis is used to refer to the release of pent up feelings and emotions in order to reduce tensions and anxieties (e.g. when individuals play competitive sport), echoing Plato's premise that a cathartic experience involves 'removing the bad, and leaving the good'. On the other hand it used to signify a purgative or liberating leisure experience accomplished through performing challenging and often distressing activities (e.g. completing a marathon).

In relation to more regulated play, there are a number of important distinctions which emerge from Callois's thesis. These are summarized by Haywood *et al.* (1995: 16–17) who argue that Callois provides an important model for understanding the functions of play in modern leisure:

- All play manifests itself in the form of games and these are of four types which he classes competitions (agon); chance (alea); make-believe (mimicry); disequilibrium (vertigo).
- The ways of playing games are located on a continuum from simple to complex, which he calls childlike (*paidia*) and structured (*ludus*).

- In games, players *express themselves* in ways not readily available to them in other aspects of life.
- Games may be *corrupted* if the qualities they require are taken to excess.
- The nature of games prevalent in a society, or its subcultures, is a powerful indicator of dominant *values* in society.

Play and mimesis

As Borsay points out, mimicry in particular provides an important link between play and modern leisure activities, which are playful in the way that they 'imitate' more serious activities such as work and education. It is in their leisure that men and women can live vicariously, where they can make believe all the things that they cannot or refuse to do in their real lives. To appreciate the real import of play, this suggests, we must try to think of ourselves into a very different world from our own everyday existence. This idea is best captured in the concept of mimesis. Derived from the Greek *mimeisthai* meaning 'to imitiate', this concept, at its most basic, describes the relationship between imitative leisure forms and reality (Blackshaw and Crawford, 2009). For example, a piece of artwork is often described as a copy of something in the 'real' world, just as some sports are described as facsimiles of battles. What these two examples suggest is that mimesis both describes the products of our leisure as well as our actions in leisure. However, as Matthew Potolsky points out, mimesis is also much more than these two things; it is a concept that has taken on 'different guises in different historical contexts, masquerading under a variety of related terms and translations: emulation, mimicry, dissimulation, doubling, theatricality, realism, identification, correspondence, depiction, verisimilitude, resemblance' (2006 :1).

In all these senses mimesis is always a double. With this is mind it is possible to argue some aspects of leisure, such as following the fortunes of your favourite sports team, for example, is an apt resemblance of a double human existence, of the fortunes as your team moves through the seasons but also the sense of life, birth, death and drama that accompany this. To this extent, it might be argued that sport gives meaning to the grim and the exciting sense of the mortality of life itself.

As I demonstrate in *The Sage Dictionary of Leisure Studies* (2009), in their discussion of sport, Elias and Dunning (1986) use the concept of mimesis in two ways: first, to depict the ways in which sport elicits different emotions and second, to show how people can act out strong feelings in sport without running the risk of sanctions. As Dunning suggests, it is in sport that you 'can vicariously experience hatred and the desire to kill, defeating opponents and humiliating enemies' (1999: 27). In other words, what is normally not condoned in real life is often made acceptable in leisure situations. Taking this understanding of mimesis to another level by highlighting the mimicry implicit to 'sports-entertainment', Atkinson (2002) argues that the cultural appeal of professional wrestling is derived from the ways in which it is able to stage contrived hyper-violent athletic competition to mass audiences in ways that still feel 'sporting' and maintain the excitement of 'real' sport. What Elias and Dunning's understanding of mimesis perhaps overlooks is the persistence of real violence in sport. For example, some people continue to pursue blood sports because they obviously enjoy hunting animals and killing them. What this suggests is that, for some people, mimesis is simply not enough and the 'hot' blood of the hunt is some kind of compensation for the 'cold' bloodiness of modern life.

Leisure, then, is an extraordinary meeting place of the real and the unreal, and it is also – what is not perhaps exactly the same thing – an extraordinary meeting place of the serious and superficial, and this is what captures its fundamental ambivalence. As an illustration of this argument, Borsay contrasts the difference between eating as a functional activity and eating as leisure, for example, at a dinner party. Here there exists the potential for cultural discourse: where the enjoyment of good food and drink is accompanied by the mutual contentment of sociability through conversation. Agnes Heller suggests that such instances of leisure effectively constitute 'other worlds', because they are fictions shared among friends and it is this that makes them concrete. In other words, these leisure situations are realities in which the real and the unreal, the serious and the superficial, come together. It is here that a form of utopia is made tangible – if 'only under the condition of the partial suspension of the pragmatic, the theoretical, and the practical pursuits in life' (Heller, 1999: 133).

Liminality, communitas and anti-structure

Looked at in this way, it might be said that leisure is a special art of arrangement or an ordering of life that exists outside time as we conventionally understand it. This is best captured in the ideas of liminality, communitas and anti-structure. The trio appears in the seminal work of Victor Turner

(1973) on pilgrimage processes. The concept of liminality, derived from the Latin word 'limen' (meaning literally a 'threshold'), connotes the idea of the 'betwixt and the between' or a place of movement 'in and out of time'. As expounded in the work of Turner, liminality describes the indefinable social and spiritual locations involved in religious rites of passage. This is also a perennial concept in the study of leisure, where it is most usually identified with rituals common to shared experiences, such as those found at carnivals, rock concerts and sports events, that signal a 'spatial separation from the familiar and habitual' and which in the process open up channels of communication to create cultural domains that transcend the limitations of class, gender, race, nationality, politics, religion, or even geography. Insights gleaned from the work of Turner suggest that liminal domains may well have a powerful cosmological significance, conveyed largely through the emotions to affirm an alternative (dis)order of things, which stress 'generic rather than particularistic relationships'.

Turner describes the shared experiences of liminality through the concept of communitas, which not only entertains cultural and social difference, but also 'strains towards' an openness that provides a 'return' to the social group denied by the manifest inequalities inherent to bourgeois society. In much the same manner of Maffesoli (1996), Turner insists that the concept of *communitas* surpasses and subverts the utilitarian and rationalistic structures of society, finding expression in 'a very concrete and communal unmediated communication between people, which it is suggested, arises spontaneously within groups sharing a similar commitment or position' (Thompson, 1981: 6). The philosopher James Carse (2008) distinguishes this concept from *civitas*, this being an unbending and defensive kind of community, while *communitas* tends to be much more open-minded and borne out of collective delight. Communitas is captured within situations of liminal 'margin' and 'remains open and specialized, a spring of pure possibility as well as the immediate realization of release from day-to-day structural necessities and obligatoriness', (Turner, 1973: 217) and often involves a startling plunge into collective sensuality that invokes mysterious depths, where the world is reflected upside down.

The carnivalesque

This idea is best illustrated in the idea of the carnivalesque, which is a blanket term that refers to those traditional, historical and enduring forms of social ritual, such as festivals, fairs and feasts, that provide sites of 'ordered disorder' (Stallybrass and White 1986), where social rules are broken and subverted; and where we can explore our 'otherness' through our instinct for life (Eros) (Freud, 1950): 'Excessive drinking, loss of inhibition, sexual immorality, mock figures of authority (such as lords of misrule and boy bishops), cross-dressing, the donning of animal costume, discordant noise, have been associated with the carnival' (Borsay, 2006: 226).

Notwithstanding its radical nature, however, the carnivalesque leaves undisturbed the normative order associated with 'real' life. On the one hand carnival experiences remain just what they are, only liminal experiences, and on the other, those aspects of them that give rise to our experimentation with 'otherness' and which challenge the status quo and do not survive the return to 'normality'. As Merton (1973) points out, social patterns have many consequences and a complex society such as ours is ultimately affected by them in myriad ways, often, and sometimes paradoxically, benefiting some social groups more than others. Consequently, those who benefit most from the maintenance of the status quo ultimately benefit more from the carnivalesque, because their powerful social positions remain radically unaltered.

The other equally pressing issue with regard to the carnivalesque is that it often manifests itself with a propensity to undermine the moral universe of the 'real' world. This might more often than not only be on a temporary basis, but the carnivalesque is nonetheless open to possibilities of disorderly activities that affect some social groups disproportionately more than others. This raises a number of ethical questions. For example, ecstatic manifestations of the carnivalesque such as parties are often associated with excessive drugs or alcohol, which raises questions about people's health. Equally they are often also fraught with the possibilities of disruptive violence, which also raises questions about the effects of unlicensed revelry on vulnerable groups such as minority ethnic communities and women. This is what Rojek calls abnormal leisure.

ABNORMAL LEISURE

In *Leisure and Culture* Rojek (2000) flips Borsay's essentialist coin from Eros (the life instinct) to Thanatos (self-destructiveness or the death instinct), eliding in the process all that makes up most 'ordinary' or 'normal' leisure lives. Just as leisure is shopping, sport, going to the cinema, the slow accretion of *skholē*, and so on, as Rojek suggests, it is also serial killing, internet pornography and third-world prostitution. Building on Durkheim's theme of the society in transition, Rojek draws on the work of Bryan Turner (1984) to demonstrate the argument that with the Enlightenment what was deemed 'abnormal' behaviour now tended to be explained in terms of medical science rather than myth. Rojek stresses that with this change the medical profession takes over issues of 'abnormal' behaviour, presenting non-religious solutions – in the form of both informal and legal discourses – for all manner of 'deviant' behaviours and 'illnesses', from drug abuse to alcoholism, masturbation to prostitution. However, the key point Rojek makes here is that one consequence of this shift towards the establishment and re-enforcement of medico-legal 'truths' about 'deviance' has been that leisure studies have in the main come to accept that 'the subject of abnormal leisure is the responsibility of criminologists and medical practitioners [and that this has in turn] contributed to the legalization and medicalization of abnormal leisure' (p. 146). Offering a critical response to this state of affairs, Rojek argues that any branch of scholarly study worth its salt must take into account abnormal behaviour and he does just this by outlining the close links between abnormal leisure practice and so called ordinary, 'normal' leisure practice.

What is abnormal leisure? As I argue in *The Sage Dictionary of Leisure* (2009), the idea might be understood as the designation for all that is strange and deviant, unbridled and tempestuous, and which in many cases are likely to be infractions of the criminal law. It also constitutes the outlandish leisure pursuits that we are illicitly attracted to, but also fear and have an unwillingness to fathom, but are often nonetheless fascinated enough to try out. To this extent, abnormal leisure is the example *par excellence* of the unresolved, disturbing forms of our desires and fantasies, the hectic pleasure of which is explored to good effect by Ken Kalfus (2006) in his post-9/11 novel *A Disorder Peculiar to the Country*. This novel demonstrates how the psychology of domestic attrition stands for the paroxysm, the whole dying world of US security, as New Yorkers indulge in 'terror sex' in order to gain social advantage, and where the highest thrill is to have sex with someone who has survived the twin towers or served emergency duty in its aftermath.

Contextualizing his core argument around the concepts of liminality, edgework and surplus energy, Rojek (2000) outlines three key types of abnormal leisure: invasive, mephitic and wild leisure. *Invasive leisure* focuses on abnormal behaviour associated with self-loathing and self-pity and the ways in which disaffected individuals experience anomie and personal alienation from the rest of society through drink, drug or solvent abuse in order that they can 'turn their back on reality'. *Mephitic leisure* encompasses a wide range of pursuits and activities, from mundane encounters with prostitutes to the buzz of murdering through serial killing. To this extent mephitic leisure experiences involve the individual's self-absorbed desire for gratification at the expense of others. Why Rojek calls these leisure activities and pursuits mephitic is that they are generally understood to be 'noxious', 'nasty', 'foul' and 'morally abhorrent' by most 'normal' people, because they cause major offence to the moral order of things.

Rojek's third category is *wild leisure* which involves limit-experiences through edgework, which refers to the ways people use leisure activities to deal with the 'edge' – the boundaries between order and disorder, life and death, consciousness and unconsciousness, subject and object – in the pursuit of voluntary risk taking and adventure. But very much like *mephitic leisure* it involves the individual's self-absorbed desire for instant gratification. The experience of 'limit' is the name of the game with *wild leisure* which includes deviant crowd behaviour such as rioting, looting and violence, particularly at sports events. Rojek also suggests that new technology presents individuals intent on pursuing *wild leisure* with ever more opportunities for instant gratification, typically in the form of video clips of anything from violence in sport to genocide, which present individuals with the vicarious 'delight of being deviant' (Katz, 1988).

The example of abnormal leisure *par excellence* is the dinner date in 2001 involving Armin Meiwes and Bernd Brandes. The former, passionate about eating someone, had advertised on the Cannibal Café website that he would like to meet up for dinner with someone equally passionate about cannibalism, but would like to be eaten. Diski (2009: 21) elaborates:

> The plan was that Armin and Bernd would dine on Bernd's severed penis, to be bitten off at the table for the occasion (this failed and it had to be cut off). Bernd found it too chewy, he said, so Armin put it in a sauté pan, but charred it and fed it to the dog. Later, Armin put Bernd in the bath (to marinate?), gave him alcohol and pills, read a science fiction book for three hours and then stabbed his dinner guest in the throat, hung him upside down on a meat hook in the ceiling, as any good butcher would, and sliced him into manageable portions.

In an interview given afterwards Meiwes explained how he had 'sautéed the steak of Bernd, with salt, pepper, garlic and nutmeg ... had it with Princess croquettes, Brussels sprouts and a green pepper sauce'.

It is not difficult to understand why most people would find this kind of leisure activity sickening. But what is being described here is not in itself amoral. As Rojek (2000) demonstrates in his discussion of abnormal leisure, leisure itself does not include ethics of *any* kind. It is part of the autonomy of leisure that it is able to free itself from morality. It might be distasteful to most people, but what Meiwes and Brandes were engaged in here was the hospitability of free exchange, where the pleasure of eating someone and the pleasure (and you would imagine also the pain) of being eaten, enhanced each other.

This last observation notwithstanding there is an 'ethical' divide about the relative merits of the concept of abnormal leisure in leisure studies. Criticizing Rojek's work, Cara Aitchison has argued that 'violence, abuse and violations of human rights may well play a part in exploitative leisure relations but these acts themselves are not acts of leisure – they are acts of violence and should be named and researched as such' (quoted in Rojek, 2000: 167). However, Rojek barks at the notion that we should ignore these kinds of leisure activities. Abnormal leisure may belong to the forbidden and the deadly, but it should not escape the notice of scholars of leisure that it *is* leisure all the same. Hannah Arendt coined the expression 'banality of evil' in order to bring to our attention the shocking ordinariness of such activities. In the light of Arendt's perceptive observation we can conclude that Rojek is merely tearing off leisure studies' veil of respectability to reveal what lurks in the hearts and minds of a good many men and women, which enables him to say something important about the infinite playfulness of the human mind. The mirror image this holds up to us may not be an ideal picture – it can frequently be dreadful and upsetting, and often even morally repugnant – but to reiterate, it *is* leisure all the same.

For all the strengths of Rojek's analysis, however, he does not give sufficient consideration to two important issues: on the one hand, the fact that what constitutes abnormal leisure is often complicated by the fact that it comes in commodity form, and on the other, the fact that even if leisure in, itself cannot be immoral, some abnormal leisure forms are ethically problematic, precisely because they do not involve the free exchange of hospitality. Both of these issues are dealt with by Blackshaw and Crabbe (2004).

Leisure and consumptive deviance

Drawing on the topic of sport and using the language of 'deviant' leisure, rather than abnormal leisure, Blackshaw and Crabbe argue that since the 1990s the demarcation between 'real' deviance and that which has been produced for consumption has blurred as the 'abnormal' has been turned into yet another marketable commodity. In other words, so called 'deviant' behaviour in sport is, as they put it, 'often just surface, flow and performance without the exit wounds'. This is abnormal leisure staged for consumption and the sense of the spectacular that is often involved, but also the mass and the calibre of the audience for it, since it is through marketized images, 'confessionals' and rumours of celebrity 'deviance' in sport that our desires for the 'deviant' Other tend more and more to be fulfilled. In a culture in which consumption is paramount, consuming 'deviant' sport becomes yet another life-style choice. The consumption of 'deviance', or what Blackshaw and Crabbe call 'consumptive deviance', seeks to capture a sense of the phantasmagoric nature of existence which eludes people in the mundane quotidian of their everyday lives. These phantasmagoria, they suggest, have become part of the high altar of consumer capitalism.

In other words, consumer capitalism now 'needs' irrationality, abnormal behaviour and impulse, and as such, the concept of abnormal leisure simply reflects the dynamics of our contemporary lived condition – it is, paradoxically, the norm. Drawing on the work of Bauman (2000a), they argue that today the 'solid' conventions associated with Freud's concept of the 'reality principle' which involved forsaking the irrational and postponing pleasure through the constant suppression of the desire for the transgressive and the 'deviant', might be considered to have been replaced by a 'precarized' hybrid existence which is both more intense but at the same time much less sure, lacking a distinctive singular feel. Since whilst the label of abnormal was easily applied in the producer based capitalism of 'solid modernity' – with its requirement for self-discipline through the values of Protestant work ethic – in the era of 'liquid' consumer capitalism the ideal consumer is not a coherent and self-disciplined *individual* with a fixed identity, but somebody who can identify with an endless supply of commodity goods. This is somebody who is also always open to new desires and new fantasies including the seductive allure of abnormal leisure which nourishes the desiring and fantasizing impulses which are both acknowledged and necessary to sustain the mediated capitalist consumer-based economy.

What this suggests is that today abnormal leisure might also be considered as something that provides consumers with a passport, which allows them to transgress relatively safely the boundaries of the permissible, allowing unmitigated access to what is conventionally repressed or forbidden. Rojek (2000: 191) argues that this kind of abnormal leisure turns us into shock-connoisseurs, seeking the next thrill, as we 'play at being deviant and engage in what Katz (1988) describes as "the delight of being deviant"'. It is the vicarious sense of having done something bad that feels rather cool that matters. In other words, the dangerous enjoyment people get from abnormal leisure doesn't just capture the euphoria of 'deviancy', it also provides the romance of it.

Heterotopic leisure

A good example for explaining this kind of abnormal leisure is the concept of heterotopia, which I discuss in the book *Key Concepts in Community Studies* (Blackshaw, 2009b). This idea is found in the work of Michel Foucault who defines it by contrasting heterotopias with utopias, which present themselves as alternative ways of living in a perfected form. According to Foucault (1984a), while this ultimately renders utopias 'unreal' places or spaces, it nonetheless means they can be contrasted with heterotopias, which are 'real' places 'without geographical markers' found in all societies and cultures. These heterotopias effectively constitute liminal 'counter-sites' of concrete utopia, which in the forms they take paradoxically lie outside all other places in any given society or culture, while nonetheless being actually localized in the already existing reality.

Foucault identifies two main categories of heterotopia. There are the pre-modern heterotopias of crisis, otherwise known as 'elsewhere' places which tended to be relegated to the margins of modern societies. Foucault has in mind here privileged places such as single-sex boarding schools where young boys are taken through a particular rite of passage; sacred places such as pilgrimage sites; and forbidden places such as brothels, where people visit prostitutes for sex. In assessing the ways in which these 'elsewhere' places have been transformed in modern societies, Foucault offers his second category of heterotopia, which at their most basic are the places of abnormal behaviour, such as prisons and mental asylums, where those considered abnormal by the standards of modern norms can be spatially isolated.

In developing a more elaborate conception of this second category of heterotopia, Foucault's analysis suggests that these places of abnormality must be understood in relation to the kind of society in which they occur. In modern societies, Foucault suggests, heterotopias have the ability to juxtapose what might conventionally be seen as several contradictory spaces into a single real place. They exist in *pointillist* time, which means they are experienced as episodic. Heterotopias also contain within these sequestered spaces their very own systems of 'opening and closing' that both isolate them from the rest of society and operate to exclude those who do not have the necessary credentials to enter. Last but not least, heterotopias, like all other communities, function by way of opposition; that is they have a tendency to unfold 'between two extreme poles'. However, heterotopias offer spaces of compensation (rather than the illusion of utopia) that function in relation to the way that their (deviant) populations understand they are imagined by the rest of society.

Foucault's work raises the key question as to why some men and women seem to want to abandon the centre and the real for the remote and the imaginary in their leisure. What his analysis also suggests is that a sense of recompense for a life that is not being lived in the confines of a modern society leads people down the track of heterotopia: reality and rationality are not on their menus, since what they are after is an unmediated immediacy of something all together out of the ordinary. What it also suggests is that if imagining community often invests in the pursuit of the ideal and embodies particular dreams, it is also given to the melancholic as well as the optimistic, the toxic as well as the beatific. In Foucault's concept of heterotopias these 'positive' and 'negative' imaginings get mixed up with one another.

In their book, Blackshaw and Crabbe (2004) provide a good example of how heterotopias operate in leisure through their research into car cruising. They argue that car cruising is an abnormal leisure activity with its own kind of detached existence, of being 'in' but not 'of' the space it temporarily occupies, and which is capable of transforming ordinary life into a form of theatre. They also contend that car cruising is a 'deviant' leisure activity as much without a history as it is one without a future and that car cruises are imaginary communities, whose inspiration tends to spring from the performativity of individual cruisers: they are both events for consumption and things to be consumed by. The affiliation found at cruises is not really one of friendship, or of a community proper, but one of symbiosis and its only glue is cruisers' insatiability for their chosen devotional leisure practice.

Summary

What the forgoing discussion suggests is that quite simply abnormal leisure is a significant concept beside itself. It acts as a vehicle which transmits the fears, fetishisms and fantasies of the contemporary world: the uneasy fascination with the irrational, our obsessions and morbid interests with violence, the confessional and all the other desires and activities which make life worth living – all of those things which reveal the immoral and aesthetic thrill of wrong doing at the moment of their revelation. And what is more, abnormal leisure also provides us with a distorting lens of the gaze through which we can look at the Other and ourselves, scoprofilic, hardly recognizable. What the discussion of heterotopias also demonstrates specifically is that what people are often looking for in their leisure these days are simply places where they can for the time being express 'abnormal' interests and identities with others similarly minded. Through sport, in particular, Blackshaw and Crabbe (2004) argue, it is also possible to pursue the Other, from the ritualized and largely socially acceptable extremes of base jumping, white water rafting and sky diving, through the legitimized violence of the rugby field, boxing ring and ice hockey arena and ultimately to the more abhorrent and pernicious forms of crime against the vulnerable, such as sexual abuse.

What all of this suggests is that the idea of abnormal leisure defies easy categorization. And the view that Blackshaw and Crabbe develop in their book suggests that, if we are properly to understand the contingently constituted nature of abnormal leisure, we must also be able to see the 'world as it is' from the context in which it takes place. In other words, the world of abnormal leisure can only be understood as a wholeheartedly contingent *set* of worlds. This is not *a* world somehow separate from the rest of society, but a series of postulated worlds in which taken for granted assumptions about *the* world we tend to understand over simply as 'reality', with its prevailing norms, values, beliefs, behaviours and actions, which are often subverted, changed or distorted. This is not an understanding of abnormal leisure in which anything goes; on the contrary it is one committed to a responsible sociology, which exposes itself to a vulnerability that Blackshaw and Crabbe argue should be the mark of all meaningful theorizing. Within this scheme of thought, instances which constitute abnormal leisure need to be *justified* empirically, theoretically and ethically. There are no God given norms and rules that underpin leisure. To reiterate: leisure itself does not include ethics of *any* kind. In adopting such an approach, leisure studies will for sure never be value-free, but then again neither will it have become valueless.

SERIOUS LEISURE VERSUS CASUAL LEISURE

From Borsay's (2006: 7) 'mutually supportive and inter-dependent pack-age' definition with its three essential elements to Rojek's debauched understanding of leisure's abnormal qualities, the discussion developed in this chapter so far has, in the main, been conspicuous by its absence of any reference to those types of activities that Robert Stebbins in various publications (1992; 1997; 1999; 2006) calls serious leisure. This is the term he uses interchangeably with casual leisure in an attempt to get to grips with a fast changing world in which work appears to be becoming less meaningful for a significant number of people. For Stebbins (1999), casual leisure is in the main consumptive and involves largely non-productive leisure activities, such as 'hanging around', drinking and smoking. Serious leisure, on the other hand, as its nomenclature suggests, is essentially a form of leisure participation that is 'craftsman-like' and built on the idea of the entitlement to enjoy the products of one's own labour. In other words, serious leisure is associated with depth and substance, while casual leisure is associated with shallowness and superficiality.

Stebbins (1999) discusses three types of serious leisure: amateurism, hobbyist pursuits and volunteerism. In his view, each of these has a special capacity to support enduring careers of leisure, which are marked by historical turning points and stages of achievement. Serious leisure also tends to be built on the kind of perseverance, which although at times might be experienced as particularly challenging for those involved, enables its participants to build special skills and knowledge; this in turn tends to engender self-confidence through achievement when they are successful. There are also other long-lasting benefits to be had through engaging with serious leisure that go beyond individual personal self-enhancement, such as material products and long-lasting personal relationships.

Perhaps the best examples of Stebbins' idea of serious leisure are craft hobbies. The word 'crafts', derived from the old English, meaning skills, refers to a particular set of abilities that are driven by human curiosity, unhurriedness and dedication to a job well done. What this suggests is that craftsmanship is creative only because it is facilitated by a particular kind of leisureliness. As Richard Sennett (2008) has suggested, what is also craftsmanlike is 'the desire to do something for its own sake', which epitomizes the special human condition of being engaged. Sennett argues that three abilities are the basis of craftsmanship: the ability to localize, the ability to question, and the ability to open up. When these three elements are combined men and women are capable of producing artifacts which are not only of stunning quality, but which also carry with them the key to their production. Craftsmanship also brings with it the capacity to endow the lives of men and women with meaning.

In all of his most recent work Sennett has been concerned with developing these kinds of ideas to explore the extent to which people lack the cultural anchor of a more coherent and secure work existence. In the concluding part of his book of lectures, *The Culture of the New Capitalism* (2005), he offers three critical values that might just fill this void: narrative, usefulness and craftsmanship. As Scruton (2008) points out, Sennett is here continuing the critique which emerged in the nineteenth century, when commentators such as John Ruskin and William Morris extolled the crafts located in people's surnames (Smith, Cartwright, Thatcher, Mason, etc.) while at the same time criticizing the industrial labour process which was replacing them.

As Sennett (2003) points out, *narratives* are an essential part of what it means to be human and are repeated and retold by men and women in different ways. Narrative identities, like the stories which underpin them, are always accompanied by their own turning points and pursuits and dreams and desires, but the time frames associated with the 'new capitalism' deprive men and women of this type of narrative movement, particularly in the workplace. In developing his critique of this situation, Sennett argues that the state has a key legitimating role to play in civil society and drawing on the idea of social capital and the critical social value of status, argues that it needs to move beyond its current merely enabling function in order to play a key role in prompting *usefulness* as a public good. Finally, drawing on Maslow's (1968) hierarchy of needs model, Sennett recommends reasserting the idea of *craftsmanship* as a key aspect of achieving fulfilment in the workplace.

It might be argued that from the perspective of leisure studies Sennett's analysis over-emphasizes the significance of work at the same time as underestimating the extent to which people today already achieve narrative coherence, usefulness and craftsmanship in their lives through serious leisure and that perhaps it does not make sense to treat work and leisure as binary opposites any longer. Notwithstanding these observations, what Sennett has to say has some real import for thinking about the implications of the ostensible demise of craftsmanship (and by default serious leisure) and the concomitant rise of consumerism and casual leisure and what this implies for the ability of individuals to embrace the autonomy and the opportunities that come with experiencing leisure that is craftsman-like and slow burn rather than consumerist and all too fleeting.

As I have argued elsewhere (Blackshaw and Crabbe, 2004; Blackshaw and Crawford, 2009), as Rojek (2000: 18) observes, serious leisure is built on a strong sense of moral foundations of social behaviour and tends to give primacy to integrative dimensions of companionship and community. In this sense, serious leisure plays a largely integrative function and as such should be understood as 'a vehicle for the cultural and moral reaffirmation of communities as places in which the individual recognizes relations of belonging'. In this regard, Stebbins takes the debate about leisure in a new direction from other more conventional approaches which largely tend to focus their critical gaze on the dichotomy between work and leisure. However, there are some problems with his analysis.

As Rojek (p.19) goes on to point out, Stebbins' fondness for serious leisure tends to 'emphasize the integrative effect of leisure in reinforcing the social order', at the expense of recognizing the efficacy of casual leisure for individuals and social groups. As he concludes Stebbins ends up reducing serious leisure to a 'rational-purposive activity'. To this extent his use of the concept has a conservative bias and is underpinned by the tacit functionalist assumption that its contribution to the larger whole of social life makes serious leisure a 'good' thing. Stebbins is simply setting up a polarity – careful creativity against carefree consumerism – and making his own allegiance clear in the process: those who pursue only casual leisure activities are unable to weigh immediate gratification against the pleasures of achievement through prolonged engagement with a leisure activity.

Another problem with Stebbins' work is that it has little to say about the different ways in which voluntary associations, such as sport and leisure clubs, operate in terms of power relations. Drawing on the work of Max Weber, Siisiäinen (2000) suggests that as well as being oligarchic and bureaucratic, many voluntary organizations are framed by internal conflicts as well as external conflicts with outsiders. In terms of the former he identifies the particular problem with top-down domination from the leadership to rank-and-file members. In relation to both internal and external power relations, I would add to this argument the point that sport and leisure associations, and long established ones in particular, are often inward looking and conservative. In marked contrast, it is in its very lack of conservatism that we find casual leisure's moral aspect: it is by and large democratic, and open to all-comers.

On a more broadly philosophical basis, Stebbins' claims for the originality for the 'serious leisure' perspective have to be called into question. The concept can be traced back to *skholē* in Plato's Republic, where Plato's 'serious play' or 'playful seriousness' provides the source for much discussion on the threats that mimesis (e.g. leisure activities such as painting, play, poetry, and such like) poses to knowledge and truth. Plato 'seriously' deplored imitators because imitations are realities that interfere with the generation of character in the guardians of society who have 'true' knowledge. Indeed, by his very disposition the imitator lacks knowledge and truth. Speaking through the character of Socrates, Plato asks:

> Do you suppose a man were able to make both, the thing to be imitated and the phantom, he would permit himself to be serious about the creating of phantoms and set this at the head of his own life as the best thing he has?
> (cited in Potolsky, 2006: 24)

Another direct link from Stebbins' work is to the *Timaeus,* an imaginative interpretation of the world's creation by a 'craftsman' who modelled his work on the Forms (e.g. ideas surrounding authenticity, pleasure, good, truth, justice, and such like). In both regards Stebbins fails to consider the extent to which his celebration of serious leisure is itself ironic, since it might be argued that what amateur, hobbyist and volunteerist pursuits are themselves is simply approximations which merely imitate (rather than initiate) the values propounded by the idea of serious leisure.

As we saw, Stebbins chooses to present the world of leisure as a Manichean confrontation between serious leisure and casual leisure; setting serious leisure up as the champion of demanding leisure against casual leisure as consumerism. For Stebbins, people are either fundamental about their leisure or they approach it without any passion that you can put a finger on. However, as well as ignoring the fact that what many people want from their leisure is just to get along with everyone else who is involved and have a bit of fun in the process, this ignores serious leisure pursuits that are not amateur, hobbyist or voluntary. Let us look at an example that does not fit neatly into Stebbins' model.

Extreme leisure

Perhaps the most obvious example is extreme leisure. From the Latin *extrēmus*, the word 'extreme' signifies something at its outermost limits. When used in conjunction with leisure it appears to have one of two meanings. The first is the idea that individuals experience certain leisure situations differently because these bring them to the limit of their resources as human beings. Examples of this kind of extreme leisure include: abnormal leisure (Rojek, 2000); barebacking or unprotected anal intercourse in episodic sexual encounters among same-sex attracted men (Ridge, 2004); dangerous leisure (Olivier, 2006); edgework (Lyng, 1990; 2005); extreme sport (Le Breton, 2000); life-style sport (Wheaton, 2004); risk recreation (Robinson, 1992); and risk sport (Breivik, 1999).

What all of these examples share in common is the idea that extreme leisure may lead to an encounter with some kind of transcendence beyond the limit of ordinary life situations, suggesting that there is something about leisure in its extreme forms that is profoundly revelatory of the human condition. The second meaning emerges from Baudrillard's work on hyperreality, which links extreme leisure with the idea of the postmodern obsession with the 'more real than real', in other words, not the beckoning hand of some alternative reality, but merely the allure of the spectacle of the consumer society performing itself through anything from extreme sport to extreme cuisine to extreme pornography.

What is most often overlooked in discussions is the politics of extreme leisure. As Laviotte (2006) argues, extreme leisure presents an ideal means for developing creative forms of radical political subversion. Through his ethnographic research into 'surfing against sewage', Laviotte explores how a surf culture in Cornwall in the UK uses extreme subversion as part of their environmental campaigns to protect the ecological sustainability of coastal leisure pursuits. Other research shows that developments in extreme leisure are just as radical but far less benign. As Franck Michel (2006) demonstrates, for example, sex tourism is a form of extreme leisure whose body trade is rooted in prostitution, and not only that, but it is also an extension of the service aspect of mass tourism that is in itself a modern version of colonial exploitation.

Like edgework, the idea of extreme leisure is open to two other major criticisms. First, innumerable numbers of people have engaged in extreme leisure activities without ever encountering an authentic self or changing their understanding of themselves in some way. Baudrillard (2001) goes as far as to suggest that all extreme forms of leisure are merely nostalgic artificial re-creations of the life and death situations which were once the human fate but have since been ameliorated with the modern civilizing process (Elias, 1994). Second, in reserving their interest for the 'limit', the 'edge', or borders of everyday existence, analysts (and participants) of extreme leisure simply fail to consider what it is that is at life's centre.

Leisure that is good of its kind

What this discussion of extreme leisure demonstrates is that there is a bad logic in trying to divide leisure into the two categories of serious leisure and casual leisure. As we have seen, because of its committed nature, it would appear that extreme leisure is a leisure practice on a par with the hobbiest pursuits identified by Stebbins. However, it is also marked by the kind of instant gratification Stebbins associates with casual leisure practices, such as shopping. Richard Hoggart (1973) offers an alternative approach to classifying leisure which suggests that if we are going to make distinctions these should be between family resemblances – distinctions which make qualified *active* judgement rather than the application of a fixed scale. In other words, you can only judge leisure within its own kind e.g. rock climbing is a category of leisure that is different from ballroom dancing. What this suggests is what is 'good of its kind' can only be determined by those for whom a particular leisure form is a devotional practice. To restate what I said in the introduction to this book, in the language game known as leisure, there are no ontologically superior concepts.

CONCLUSION

This chapter has looked at three conceptual approaches for understanding leisure: the essential elements of leisure; abnormal leisure; and serious and casual leisure. The following conclusions can be drawn from the discussion.

One way in which leisure can be defined is through the three elements of symbolism, play and 'other', which are highly conspicuous in our leisure activities, are present in a specific combination, and our need for them in this combination appears to be a historical constant. What this discussion revealed is that the context in which leisure takes place is important and that it might best be understood as a special art of arrangement or an ordering of life that exists outside time as we conventionally understand it, and as such is an extraordinary meeting place of the real and the unreal and the serious and superficial, and this is what captures its fundamental ambivalence. This discussion also revealed a number of related concepts for understanding leisure – notably pleasure, desire and happiness; mimesis; liminality, communitas and anti-structure; and the carnivalesque – while highlighting and discussing their strengths and limitations.

One general conclusion emanated from the discussions of abnormal leisure and serious versus casual leisure and that is that if leisure is infinitely variable, acquiring a new identity in the mind of every new participant, it is always in both the intimate world of private life and the public world of culture, subject to the ever-changing human landscape in which it moves. The discussion of these two perspectives also revealed a number of other concepts for understanding leisure, including consumptive deviance, heterotopic leisure and extreme leisure.

The discussion of abnormal leisure confirmed that leisure itself does not include ethics of *any* kind, but when people freely engage in leisure together they establish their own ethics. The main specific conclusion to be drawn from the discussion of serious leisure versus casual leisure was that if we are going to make value judgements about leisure it is conceptually more rigorous to use the 'good of its kind' rule.

In sum, we may say that if leisure is a historical constant it can be defined neither in exclusively essentialist terms nor without taking into account the fact that it is a social and cultural phenomenon which is always subject to change and that it must be interrogated with this in mind.

Part II

LEISURE IN HISTORICAL AND SOCIAL THOUGHT

3

THE ANTECEDENTS OF MODERN LEISURE

The history of modern leisure is about 400 years long and we do not have the space in the confines of this chapter to discuss this in any depth. For those readers whose interest in investigating modern leisure is purely a historical one, I recommend that they consult Peter Borsay's (2006) *A History of Leisure: The British Experience since* 1500. Borsay's book is important since, as Rojek (1985: 24) points out, most other general histories of modern leisure have a tendency to adopt the period of industrialization as 'the central time-unit for study' (Malcolmson, 1973; Bailey, 1978; Cunningham, 1980; Walton and Walvin, 1983). However, this endeavour to locate a source for modern leisure in industrialization should not surprise us since as Clarke and Critcher assert, 'looking at trends evident by the 1840s, the clearest impression is of the wholesale changes in the rhythms and sites of work and leisure enforced by the industrial revolution (*sic*). It was during this period that what we come to see as a discrete area of human activity called "leisure" became recognisable' (1985: 58).

THE EMERGENCE OF MODERN LEISURE IN INDUSTRIAL BRITAIN

Developing a critical neo-Marxist perspective that draws on E.P Thompson's (1967) assumption that industrialization ushered in a new era of rigorous time-discipline, Clarke and Critcher 'take the view not so much that leisure was absent before the nineteenth century, but that it could not be separated from work, and was therefore effectively indistinguishable as a category of experience' (Borsay, 2006: 9). As they assert:

> The fluidity of the boundaries work and leisure was apparent in the street culture of village and town. Workshop and tavern opened side by side on to the street. Drinking, producing, bargaining, passing the time of day, all contributed to common flow, eddying around street traders, itinerant salesmen, balladeers. Here work and leisure intermingled, both aspects of a life which was, above all, *public* in its orientation and presence.
>
> (Clarke and Critcher, 1985: 53–4)

However, to argue that work and leisure were so completely de-differentiated until the nineteenth century is not entirely convincing. As Glennie and Thrift (1996: 289) point out, 'certain holidays persisted as part of recreational calendars in early modern England long after their theological justification had been explicitly abandoned'. As Ehrenreich (2007) shows, too, especially from the fifteenth century onwards, men and women in pre-industrial society demonstrated a marked facility for reinventing traditional festivals as a result of the suppression within the churches of the more exuberant forms of worship and popular forms of piety during the post-Reformation. She argues that it was during this time that festival culture really came into its own as men and women deserted the hard day-to-day drudge of work to make collective sites of 'ordered disorder'. What this suggests is that, in common with Thompson, in Clarke and Critcher's account 'the static nature of traditional holidays, calendars, and irregular working practices such as "Saint Monday"', are drastically exaggerated and are effectively treated as 'anthropological features' of pre-industrial life, rather than 'historically-specific practices' found in only certain places (Glennie and Thrift, 1996: 289).

In their most recent work, Glennie and Thrift (2009) extend their claim that this Thompsonian notion of time-discipline is 'too narrow and too contextually specific' by demonstrating that men and women in pre-industrial society might not have had to labour under the tyranny of clock time – clocking in at work and obeying railway timetables rather than the more 'natural' rhythms of their localities – but there was nonetheless a well established working week: 6am to 6pm between Tuesday to Saturday. What this meant is that there was a separate time of the week, which was the 'weekend' on Sunday and Monday. What this suggests is that even if they did not use the term 'leisure', people in pre-industrial society had a specific time-space to indulge in leisure activities outside and beyond their religious commitments and associated 'holydays'.

We can, however, make one general observation about leisure under industrialization which came out with the destruction of this pre-industrial world and this concerns the emergence of rational organization of mass leisure based on 'the accumulation and productivity requirements of the capitalist class' (Rojek, 1985: 68). In explaining this tendency scholars typically identify three major factors: the emergence of a civilizing trend (Elias, 1994) in relations between state formation and changes in individual conduct, including new guidelines of morality and controlled, ordered and self-improving leisure forms, such as 'rational recreation' and its perceived 'profits' of education and discipline (Cunningham, 1980), which became 'a slogan if not an organized movement, then a slowing diffusing mood' (Clarke and Critcher, 1985: 58); the growing significance of leisure as a definer of social status and cultural competition for *distinction* at first between the 'higher orders' and the 'lower orders', which later extended to different status groups across the social spectrum (Bourdieu, 1984); and the suppression of the threat posed by extant forms of popular culture to clock-time paid work. By the early to mid-1800s the kinds of leisure forms that popular culture had traditionally promoted – heavy drinking, dog-fighting, bull-baiting, street fighting and so on – were also increasingly seen through the eyes of establishment figures, such as employers, magistrates and Puritan reformers, as problematic, signifying in the view of some as a social class struggle over leisure (Clarke and Critcher, 1985).

One of the great merits of Clarke and Critcher's book is to show that the attacks on popular cultural pleasures were not simply the result of a collision between social class interests and a rudimentary capitalist bureaucratic state, but the continuation of a very old story concerning social and economic inequality and inequitable access to leisure. It is here that the idea of leisure as a compensatory activity is to be found: the prescribed time free from hard industrial toil available to recuperate workers in order to extract the maximum output from them when they return to the workplace. As we have seen, however, Clarke and Critcher also argue, more controversially, that leisure and work were indistinguishable from one another until the nineteenth century. In their view, the 'term "leisure" differentiates employment from free time with a sharpness which does not accord with the experience of daily life at the end of the eighteenth century' (p. 52). It was only from the middle of the nineteenth century when 'a variety of attendant developments, notably a general increase in real earnings, new technologies (railways and the steam press) and a new range of leisure forms, sites and services (from croquet to skating rinks to travel agencies) combined to give shape and growth to what historians have labelled 'a virtual leisure revolution', 'a new leisure world' (Bailey, 1989: 108). This is a world marked by 'the commercialization of leisure', which Plumb (1973) forcefully argues was both facilitated by the Industrial Revolution and was also in part responsible for it. As the consumer market for goods grew, the demand for goods exceeded capacity and new technologies of manufacture had to be developed.

The expansion of British trade in the second half of the eighteenth century also led to the development of a new kind of relationship with the world. But what the Industrial Revolution also produced was not just things – it was things to consume. This was the case for amusements and entertainments; newspapers, magazines and book; and sports, such as cricket, football and racing. New leisure experiences arrived, seemingly all of a sudden and within the financial grasp of the mass of ordinary people. Railways in the nineteenth century would also have another transformative effect on leisure – especially seaside outings, holidays and tourism – that the car and aeroplane would also have on the twentieth century. As Bailey (1989: 109) observes, by the end of the nineteenth century the world seemed 'settled into a distinctive leisure landscape', one so recognizable that it moved the leisure historian Hugh Cunningham to claim that 'there is nothing in the leisure of today which was not visible in 1880'. At the same time the social class structure functioned in much the same way it had one hundred years earlier, if in a more elaborate way: 'upper classes, characterized in the public mind in bowler hats, stately homes, land-ownership and fox-hunting; the middle classes: professional, suburban, trilby-wearing home-owners, gardeners and rugby/tennis enthusiasts; and the working-classes: urban-dwelling, council tenants and cloth-capped denizens of the pub and the football terrace' (Garnett and Weight, 2004: 100–1).

It might be helpful to sum up the thread of the discussion developed so far. In trying to account for the emergence of modern leisure, historians have by and large selected one historical period when a certain way of living had spread widely and become relatively settled as people in an industrial production-based and capitalist society made up of social hierarchies built on the work ethic and sustained by economic stratification responded to their changed circumstances. While some historians have merely tried tracing the chronology of change instigated by industrialization, especially the commercialization of leisure, others have been much more critical, arguing that the emergence of modern leisure is part and parcel of history of the class struggle. We also saw that more recent historical accounts have challenged some of the tacit assumptions made by Marxist inspired critical historical perspectives, particularly the ideas that until the nineteenth century leisure was indistinguishable from work and that time-discipline was a distinctly industrial, capitalist phenomenon.

HISTORICIZING LEISURE

What is lacking from all these accounts is any sustained discussion of the key social, cultural and political factors that gave rise to industrialization and in the process dismantled the traditional way of life and the kinds of leisure practices associated with pre-modern society. It is with the challenge of outlining and discussing these that this chapter is concerned. The best way to understand this transition, as I shall demonstrate below, is to focus not so much on the history of changes that accompanied new trends in leisure, but to account for the factors that gave rise to modern society and the emergence of leisure as a modern phenomenon. In order to do this, what I offer here is essentially a social theoretical account of the key factors that gave rise to the emergence of modernity.

It may seem to be a tautology but modern leisure must be understood as having its antecedents in the substitution of modernity for traditional society. The idea of modernity, or I should say, modernization, refers to the emergence of a new faith in the processes of scientific knowledge and technological advance which marks the beginning of modernity's separation from traditional society. Giddens argues that, regardless of the initial force of circumstances that meant that it had to conspire with its progenitor, modernity contrives to destroy the world that preceded it. For Giddens (1994: 63), tradition is a practice which is 'bound up with ... "collective memory"; involves ritual; is connected with ... a *formulaic notion of truth*'; has a supportive framework of 'saints' and 'guardians'; 'and, unlike custom, has binding force which has a combined moral and emotional content'. It is nigh on impossible to differentiate between real, invented and imagined traditions, but as Giddens shows the formulaic *notion of the truth* of tradition is a manifestation of active 'collective memory'; and as such, is forever being recreated in the present.

As Bauman (1994) suggests traditional society was a relatively coherent world and constituted an organic totality of activities and knowledge which was fully integrated into everyday life. Men and women did not merely populate their world in the modern sense; they were part of the world in which they lived and it was part of them. In this view, leisure mirrored life itself in traditional society, which was lived in a ritualistic fashion and it constituted a communal way of life to the extent that it was thought of

> as *natural*, like other 'facts of nature'; and it need not be laboriously constructed, maintained and serviced ... it is at its strongest and most secure when we believe just this: that we have not chosen it on purpose, have done nothing to make it exist and can do nothing to undo it.
>
> (Bauman, 1990: 72)

It is generally accepted that the coming of modernity, with the 'discovery' of some alternative 'universal laws' of nature and society, came into being with the Enlightenment (the age of modern reason bound to the twin ideas of rational inquiry and scientific method which emerged in the seventeenth century) and the shift from traditional society to modernity involved moving from a devotional religious world to a secular world of science. Contrary to traditional society, with modernity, *rationality* becomes, in Giddens' sense, *embedded in* the knowledge process:

> intellectually calculable rules and procedures are increasingly substituted for sentiment, tradition and rule of thumb in all spheres of activity. Rationalisation leads to the displacement of religion by specialised science as the major source of intellectual authority; the substitution of the trained expert for the cultivated man of letters; the ousting of the skilled handworker by machine technology; the replacement of traditional judicial wisdom by abstract, systematic statutory codes. Rationalisation demystifies and instrumentalises life. It means that. ... there are no mysterious, incalculable forces that come into play, but rather that one can, in principle, master all things by calculation.
>
> (Wrong, quoted in Abrams (1982: 83–4)

If traditional society was governed by predictability and certitude, modernity is inherently disorderly, experimental and go-getting since it

> means incessant, obsessive modernization (there is no state of modernity; only a process; modernity would cease being modernity the moment that

process ground to a halt); and all modernization consists in 'disembedding', 'disencumbering', 'melting the solids', etc.; in other words, in dismantling the received structures or at least weakening their grip.

(Bauman, 2004: 20)

It is, of course, impossible to be precise about the why, the when, the
where and the how of the substitution of modernity for traditional
society. At what point did the dynamic of modernity usurp the *telos* of
the pre-modern social arrangement of traditional society locked into a
timeless present, a totality marked by subsistence, casual brutality, and
ignorance of the world beyond its bounds? Who knows? Still, it would
not be too far wrong to suggest that at some point in the seventeenth
century traditional society was broken by a combination of factors that
accompanied the progress of freedom from its roots in the Reformation
and the Enlightenment: these were the large technological transforma-
tions that had their basis in the Industrial Revolution and which formed
the platform for the rise of capitalism and a society based on social class
differences.

Before we go on to look at the consequences of these seismic shifts
in the processes of history for understanding the emergence of modern
leisure, let us first of all briefly consider the precise meaning of life in the
eyes and minds of the men and women who inhabited what Heller (2005)
aptly calls the pre-modern social arrangement.

The pre-modern social arrangement

This world is reminiscent of what the philosopher Martin Heidegger
called *zuhanden gelassenheit*. It has the capacity to simply let things be what
they are, to leave them in order that they may sediment and acquire their
own intractable existence, as if they came into being of their own volition,
or by divine ruling. The *zuhanden* kind of world is

at once unchanging and arbitrary. Life must follow the ways of the past; and
at the same time life cannot be planned ... patterns of life are fixed in ways
that cannot, must not, be broken just because they are traditional; at the
same time unpredictable, unreliable, miraculous.

(Abrams, 1982: 93)

In such a world men and women are *embedded* in the dense folds of tradition. The place that they occupy in the social hierarchy is determined by

their individual function in life. So, for example, in the same way that aristocrats and the landed gentry ruled the roost in the feudal estates found in pre-modern Europe, clergymen were charged with the holy orders, and the serfs were tied to the land where they lived and worked with all too infrequent respite. As the following ideal typical summing up from Shivers and deLisle (1997: 53) demonstrates, this is a world in which

> free time was needed to rest and recuperate from the unceasing toil that feudal society demanded. It was a time of raucous activities, for letting go, singing indecent love songs, dancing around a flowery maypole, and watching a travelling show with its mumming, masques, and dancing animals. These respites were brief, but the peasants deemed themselves lucky to stay alive and asked no more than the security they received from their masters. A medieval rhyme suggests that the human order was determined by God and one should not attempt to change the system.
>
> (Shivers and deLisle, 1997: 53)

As Heller (1992: 83) points out, pre-modern men and women 'do not see beyond the horizons of their world; only their own world endures'. There would have been almost no possibilities of anyone escaping their shared fate, because it was God's will that they should stay put. In such a world social life is built on necessity. The putative harmony and order of traditional life is an imposed one – a 'mutuality of the oppressed' (Williams, 1973). As Heller (1999) points out, what this tells us is freedom as modern men and women know it is not an option in this kind of world, except for the minority who are born free and for some unlikely reason lose that freedom.

To draw on Heidegger's terminology once again, it was those seismic shifts in the processes of history that swung the pendulum of human fate from constraint to freedom – the discovery of culture, the substitution of rationality and reason for irrationality, the shift from stasis to progress, the dethroning of God and the discovery of the individual, to name just the four most striking new 'facts of life' emanating as a result of the dynamic of modernity – that, to paraphrase Bauman (2004: 8), pulled the world out of

> the dark expanse of *zuhanden* (that is 'given to hand' and given to hand matter-of-factly, routinely, and therefore 'unproblematically'), and transplanted it on to the brightly lit stage of *vorhanden* (that is, the realm of things that,

in order to fit the hand, need to be watched, handled, tackled, kneaded, moulded, made different than they are).

As Anderson (1991) has convincingly argued, these altered conditions of existence led to the collapse of three key conceptions of the world: the idea that religion offered privileged access to truth; the belief that monarchs were persons apart from the rest of humankind and somehow pre-ordained to preside over them; and an understanding of the past and the present in terms of some creation myth – three conceptions, we might add, that rooted human lives firmly in an unchanging world.

With the onset of the modern social arrangement a new era of self-determination had arrived and no longer could men and women sleep walk through their lives; from now on they had to learn how to wake themselves up and make their own destinies. This substitution of the penumbra of *zuhanden* and its stultifying confines for the searchlight and spotlights of *vorhanden* meant that there could no longer be any escape from the consequences of contingency, no return to whatever world there was before the dynamic of modernity took over. In other words, modernity had succeeded in displacing the pre-modern social arrangement and the world of tradition could never be the same again. It was kaput.

The Reformation and the Enlightenment

Any endeavour to locate a source for understanding the emergence of modernity and with it modern leisure must begin with a discussion of the Reformation and the Enlightenment. Pre-Reformation Europe was a unified Christendom whose social organization was based on common doctrines, sacraments, a common language (Latin), unity in prayer, mass universal canon law, common church structure and the spiritual primacy of the Pope. The Reformation (*circa* 1517–59) was a social, religious and political movement that began as an attempt to reform the worldly corruption of the Roman Catholic Church and resulted in the establishment of a Protestant alternative. Keith Thomas's (1975) important study *Religion and the Decline of Magic* identifies the effects of the 'purification' of the supportive framework of 'saints' and 'guardians' associated with the unified Christendom in the post-Reformation period and how these led to ascendancy of the principle of individual subjectivity, which meant that the subjective mind could discover and assert itself as *the* source of value, rather than depending on the agency of God.

There is no doubt that this societal drift towards individualization also stemmed intellectually from the Renaissance and materially from the growing economic power of the middle classes in the early modern period. It is not clear whether Foucault ever read Norbert Elias, but it appears to be Elias's (1991 *1939*) crucial observation that it is the interdependency between society shaping individuals and individuals forming their own society out of their life (including their work and leisure pursuits) that is the central feature of the modern 'society of individuals', which led him to suggest that individualization emerged once human beings began (to paraphrase Foucault) to exist within themselves, inside the shell of their heads, inside the armature of their limbs, and in the whole structure of their physiology; when they began to exist at the centre of their own labour about whose principles they were now governed by and whose product would now elude them (Foucault, 1986: 318). What Foucault is describing here is the emergence of the Enlightenment, otherwise known as the age of modern reason and justice, which brought with it a rational commitment to robust individualism and the right to freedom from religion and the state. To be human was now to suffer inner torment, to feel unsure and inadequate, to be torn between an outmoded religious belief and the desire to live as an individual *de facto*, with all the potential dangers associated with this.

As we saw in Chapter 1, Heller (2009) argues that in this way Christianity followed in the footsteps of the classical Greek world by developing its own special reading of the Bible in which it was understood that those individuals who followed the path of their desires, pleasures and emotions without proper control were regarded 'not just as inferior men, but as sinners'. Thomas takes the view that from the mid-sixteenth century onwards increased accusations of idleness seem to have been induced by this new stress on individual responsibility for the self, which in turn produced a new anxious age in which the Devil came increasingly to be seen as a suitable scapegoat on which to hang all too human failings.

The subject of the Devil was a key feature of Calvinism, one of the 'hotter types' of Puritan doctrines of the sixteenth century (Coward, 2003), named after John Calvin (1509–64), leader of the Reformation in France, which had reached Britain by 1559 (Shivers and deLisle, 1997). In the religious sphere, the influence of Calvinism expanded and was taken up by the most godly Puritans, 'who adopted a very militant attitude in seeing the English as the Elect Nation chosen by God to lead the cause of international Calvinism' (Coward, 2003: 85), in order to 'purify' the Church of England of its Catholic ceremony. This doctrine, closely bound up with Calvin's own ideas, though not limited to them, had as its primary sources: the doctrine of the 'elect' or predestination (i.e. people should know their station in life and be respectful of those in positions of authority); the idea that work is a virtue and recreation is an acceptable way of recuperating for work, but that leisure involving enjoyment for its own sake (drinking, dancing, gambling, ribaldry and so on) is simply idleness, which is likened with the work of the Devil. It is important to note, however, that what gave this crusade for

> godly reformation its zeal was not a kill-joy spirit, which seems to have been largely absent from seventeenth-century Puritanism, but instead a deeply-held conviction among the godly that without such reformation they and the nation would lose God's support and God would (as they graphically put it) 'spit in their face'.

> (ibid.: 86)

The Protestant work ethic

What the discussion developed so far suggests is that the origins of modern individual subjectivity can be found in the Reformation and the Enlightenment and modern understandings of both work and leisure are prefigured in religious change. Thomas (2009) has noted that the doctrine that work is an unpleasant and inescapable part of daily living is already prefigured in Christianity. This observation is perhaps best expressed in John Milton's masterpiece *Paradise Lost*. Published in 1667, *Paradise Lost* is an epic poem concerned with the expulsion of Adam and Eve from the Garden of Eden, which is a Christian story about the Fall of humankind. In this story, a life of labour is the unpleasant and unavoidable punishment for the sin of Adam and Eve, who, having eaten the forbidden fruit, are driven out of the door of Paradise into the new empty world before them. For this sin 'the earth had been cursed and no longer yielded its fruits willingly' (Thomas, 2009: 79) and from now on it was only through the hard toil of labour that humankind is able to reap its rewards.

The assumption of the Puritan doctrine was thus that the 'natural human impulse' is to idleness and without the supportive framework of 'saints' and 'guardians' only individual penance could pave the way to God. It was in recognition of this that Protestantism provided Christians with 'the intellectual and cultural resources to cope with a more individualistic and often precarious way of life while retaining a shared framework of meaning and sense of existential security based on religious tradition' (Cummings, 2009). This new notion of individual 'sin' brought with it self-scrutiny and rejection of worldly pleasure. For men and women in the post-Reformation era this meant more work and less leisure, because, as we have seen already, the latter was seen as irresponsible and un-godly. Work on the other hand was now understood, like religion, as a calling, and those who answered the call were different, and better people. As Thomas goes on to indicate, though, this counsel did not apply to all ranks of 'patient and persevering labourers' in the same way. Indeed, 'in the case of magistrates, ministers, "men of high degree", or those "of noble family and extraction", "sweat of the brow" was not to be taken too literally'. Indeed, it is only the poor and the powerless that have to persevere.

[I]n the toil imposed on Adam [and Eve] after the Fall; the agricultural way of life has profound religious value, for the Church portrays it as biblical punishment but equally as the means of redemption. It is ... not an accident ... that with the resurrection of Christ, who comes to free Adam and his descendants, both the fields and the men who work them also rise again.

(Frugoni, 2005: 18)

The 'Weber Thesis': the Protestant ethic and the rise of capitalism

In his classic studies of the 'Protestant ethic and the spirit of capitalism' Max Weber (1930) makes the connection between religion and work even more explicit. Weber's basic thesis is that capitalism developed from ideas borrowed from Protestantism, with him observing crucially the way in which the idea that wealth creation is virtuous drew on Puritan ideas about an 'elect', divinely privileged section of society. To the point, Protestantism (informed by the Calvinist belief in predestination and the spirituality of wealth) and the rationalization of the economy turned out to be the mutually reinforcing driving forces in developing Western capitalism. The idea that productive labour as something valued in and for itself and had a god-like significance and sense of moral obligation, was what Weber described as a Protestant ethic, which in his view, originated in the asceticism of Puritanism at the Reformation, and when combined with fiscal prudence was to become a unique feature of Western European culture. In other words, once economic life began trading on religious belief, it was the driving force behind modern industrial capital-ism, which in turn generated a clear distinction between the spheres of work and leisure (Bailey, 1978).

The major social, economic, and political factors particularized by Weber in his analysis are outlined by Giddens in the 1976 imprint of *The Protestant Ethic and the Spirit of Capitalism*. First, Giddens specifies that, although the household in traditional society was a place for work, with the development of industrial capitalism, the separation of work from the home (and leisure) soon became the norm for most people. This process was preceded by the guild and craft fellowships, which were well established in medieval Europe. Giddens notes that this process did not occur in the East, as these fellowships were not apparent. Second, in marked contrast to their Eastern counterparts, Western cities had, at the emergence of industrial capitalism, developed highly sophisticated political structures based on a 'bourgeois', rather than a traditional, feudal outlook. Third, and just the reverse to about everywhere else in the world, there existed, in Europe, 'a more integrated and developed rationalisation of juridical practice', bequeathed by the Roman Empire. Additionally, for Weber, this juridical framework was decisive in facilitating the organiza-tion of the new capitalist economy and was one crucial element in deter-mining the origins of the nation state.

Finally, what was also crucial to the transition was the establishment of double-entry bookkeeping in Europe. It turned out to be the mas-ter design in underwriting the whole capitalistic enterprise, according to Weber. Taken together, these processes forwarded the erosion of pre-modern social stratification based on feudal estates and paved the way for a new form of social stratification based on social class lines, where the masses were now 'free' to sell their wage-labour. As Giddens points out, the caste systems of China and India, for example, proved to be more enduring than feudal estates; and this again played a major part in differ-entiating the East from the European experience.

In sum, Weber argued that along with the institutional dimensions described above, the 'Protestant ethic' played a key role in bringing about this monumental historical transition. Quoting Weber, Rojek (1995: 46) argues that life now had to be spent 'not in leisure and enjoyment, but only in activity [which] serves to increase the glory of God'. What Rojek fails to point out, however, is that what Weber also argued, crucially, but equally as controversially, was that the religious facet of this affirmation of the virtues of hard daily work was soon extinguished by the very ethic it had produced. In other words, God's calling to humankind's work role in society was no longer necessary to Western capitalism once it had become established, because labour could be 'performed as if it was an absolute end in itself'.

The 'Weber Thesis' has been widely criticized on the basis that it lacked a solid empirical base, especially its author's neglect of the influences and changes contiguous with Catholicism. The fact that the ability of industrial capitalism to sustain itself was dependent on the consumption of commodities, as well as a willingness to forgo immediate pleasures and planning for the future hardship, and Weber's propensity to overlook the fact that, if Protestantism was a religion of great variety, it was nonetheless in many ways at odds with nascent industrial capitalism (Tawney, 1958; Green, 1959; George and George, 1961; Samuelsson, 1961; Elton, 1963).

Notwithstanding these criticisms there is no doubt that the Protestant work ethic was the attitudinal base on which Western capitalism developed and the implications of this for understanding modern leisure. As Borsay (2006: 14) asserts in his assessment of the historical evidence:

> Though any crude notion of a sudden Protestant crackdown on pleasure is difficult to sustain, there appears a long-term but uneven and highly contested process of attrition by which England was deprived of some of its traditional merry-making. ... Such a valorization of work did not necessarily imply a wholesale abandonment of leisure. However, it did require a reassessment of how work, leisure and religion – and indeed, education, civil life, and ordinary life – interacted.

What this suggests is that the Protestant work ethic was always from the beginning very much a social and cultural phenomenon rather than a stringently religious one.

Paradise Lost – again

For all the final triumph of the Reformation, which the Puritans worked so hard to promote, it is another, perhaps more important, message that emerges from Milton's *Paradise Lost* that spread deeper through the modern social world and popular culture than even the Protestant work ethic, taking root in the minds of individuals with little or no religious faith. In other words, men and women did not turn to Protestantism for 'a shared framework of meaning and sense of existential security' in order to cope with individualization, but to the community. Indeed, as Milton demonstrates, humankind's love affair with community also begins with Adam and Eve, who, having eaten the forbidden fruit, are driven out of the door of Paradise into the new empty world before them. If physical self-consciousness is the first symptom of their exit, this is quickly followed by the recognition that some mistakes are irredeemable and that Paradise will always be lost, and regretted, that the present cannot be escaped, and that from this point onwards Adam and Eve will have to make their own lonely way through life, either together or apart – the choice is individually their own. As Milton (1968: 292) puts it in the closing lines of *Paradise Lost*:

> The world was all before them, where to choose
> Their place of rest, and Providence their guide.
> They, hand in hand with wand'ring steps and slow,
> Through Eden took their solitary way.

Adam and Eve have two options: they can either look back nostalgically at Paradise in the hope that if they look hard enough they will find all the fragments of its broken totality, and that if they can put these back together without any cracks, that what has vanished might reappear, that the scattered shards and dust of Paradise might be reunited by a word, that something consumed by the fire of human curiosity might be made to sprout forth once again from a pile of ash. Milton, the champion of Cromwell's republican movement, knows that this is an illusion. The true magic of *Paradise Lost* lies in the ability of the world it contained to vanish, to become so thoroughly lost, that it might never have existed in the first place. The enduring message of Milton's poem is that if men and women are prepared to support one another beyond Paradise from which they have been forever exiled, they will begin to recognize that they have the world 'all before them'.

In other words, humankind might have been exiled from the old traditional world of certainty, but it has the opportunity to make a new kind of secular Paradise in the modern world. The archangel Michael tells Adam and Eve as they leave the Garden of Eden that if they practise Christian virtues, they will find Paradise *within* themselves. Christianity's teleological foundation has metamorphosed into a never-ending homelessness, a fate at once both acknowledged and resisted by a modern imagination nourished on faith. As Claire Tomalin (2008) has suggested, Milton has to be read as a 'man full of ideas that are sometimes in conflict with each other'. Indeed, Milton's ideas emerge from a Christian foundation but will not be bound by it; he is too greatly attached to Christianity's hermeneutical tendencies to purge himself of its dictates. In the event, the central message emerging from *Paradise Lost* must also be read as secular in spirit: community emerges from a Christian base but is no longer bound by it. Men and women freed from the shackles of religion need not feel nostalgic about *Paradise Lost* since they have the gift to find Paradise amongst themselves, and with it the potential to be 'happier far' than they ever were in Eden.

The Miltonic duality of leisure

Step into the mid-nineteenth century pub and you find yourself transported into a firmly entrenched working-class world. By this time pubs had become

> the great social centres of working-class life, their attractions based upon, but also reaching far beyond the consumption of alcohol. Some turned themselves into informal working-men's clubs where friendly societies, trade unions, and craft societies met in upstairs rooms. Until 1886 (when children under 13 were banned) all ages were welcome, though after 1839 spirits could not be sold to those under 16. Election campaigns were planned in pubs and susceptible voters 'treated' to drinks. Freemasons and dog fanciers met in pubs. Publicans were more often the patrons of local sporting events than parsons or ministers. Pubs constituted the quickest route to oblivion, but they also provided a 'good time' – 'beano', 'spree', and 'blow-out' were all popular mid-Victorian terms. Small wonder that, according to an estimate of 1853, 70 per cent of working men in Derby passed their evenings in pubs. Small wonder that many families must have spent a third and some half or more of all their income on drink … Not unrepresentative was the slum pub observed in late nineteenth-century York: a shabby parlour accommodating ten drinkers, no music, bleak décor – but, despite the presence of thirteen other pubs within five minutes' walk, still able to attract 550 customers on a typical day, of whom (pubs were never all-male affairs) only 258 were men.
>
> (Hoppen, 1998: 355–6)

As this quotation demonstrates the history of leisure is about living, breathing people, not abstract Puritan doctrines. But in the breadth of its insights and vigour of its prose, *Paradise Lost* reveals the two major influences on leisure that lie beneath the key social, cultural, economic and political changes brought about by modernity: on the one hand the cold comfort of compensatory leisure against the grim Protestant work ethic and on the other the warm communal togetherness of popular cultural pastimes against cold lonely individualism. In other words, what we find with the emergence of modernity is the coexistence of a Miltonic legacy: Milton the Puritan and Milton the Utopian.

You could go as far as to argue that every aspect of modern leisure turns in one way or another on Milton's legacy, however diluted and de-Christianized: from the ways which present day 'moral entrepreneurs' (Becker, 1963) respond to everyday legal leisure activities, such as the drinking of alcohol, sex, and television and video game violence, as if they were entries to sin, to the contemporary obsession with community, which as I have argued elsewhere is encountered everywhere these days, and especially in the leisure domain (Blackshaw, 2009b). As we saw in the last chapter, however, there are some in society, nowadays, that seem to prefer their visions of community leisure under the auspices of quite another kind of authority, heterotopia, in fact, as imagined, not by John Milton, but by Michel Foucault. As we will see in Chapter 6, though, there are some other stories that we also like to continue to tell about the present world that favour this Miltonic duality, but these emerge in commodity form and with an ironic twist. In Chapter 5 we shall explore the postmodern conditions that give rise to such sentiments and sensibilities, but before that we need to look in more detail at leisure in so far as it is a social phenomenon characterized by social divisions and inequalities of opportunity. This is the topic of the next chapter.

CONCLUSION

In this chapter leisure was looked at first of all historically. It was shown that the history of leisure is as a rule the history 'concentrated on the nineteenth century, and its interpretations of social change and the role of leisure in the formation and mediation of class cultures' (Bailey, 1989: 107). After we identified and exposed some of the limitations of historical leisure studies, we historicized the idea of leisure by extracting it from the conventional historical practice of outlining its chronology to tracing its antecedents in the substitution of modernity for the pre-modern social arrangement. In this discussion, the Reformation and the Enlightenment emerged as the two key reference points for the development of human subjectivity and individualization, which together produced a new anxious Puritan age. It was demonstrated by discussing one of the 'hotter types' of Puritanism, Calvinism, that if Puritanism was social and cultural rather than a stringently religious phenomenon, it also did not apply to all classes of people in the same way. Through a discussion of Weber's (1930) classical study, it was also demonstrated how Puritanism combined with capitalism in a dialectical way to form a modern society underpinned by the Protestant work ethic and that the emergence of modern leisure must be understood in the light of this. Finally, it was argued that if Milton's *Paradise Lost* can be read as an elegy which also enables us to account for the cold comfort of compensatory leisure against the grim Protestant work ethic, it is also one which enables us to explain the significance in industrial modernity of warm communal togetherness of popular cultural pastimes against cold lonely individualism.

4

ANALYSING LEISURE AS A
SOCIAL PHENOMENON

In the first three chapters of this book the reader was presented with what may well have seemed like a bewildering, if fascinating, variety of leisure concepts, displaying some clear family resemblances as well as some of their own distinctive characteristics. As was pointed out in the introduction, this should in itself not be surprising since the world of leisure does not, as you might say, naturally carve itself into objects. It only becomes meaningful because of how and where we deploy its 'rules of grammar', in accordance with 'language games' of the various everyday situations in which we find ourselves. We could of course stop there, and treat the understanding of leisure we have developed so far as normative, in no way to be challenged. However, that would go against the protocols of *skholē* and the critique underpinning this book. As it was demonstrated in the last chapter what we need to continually bear in mind is that our thinking about leisure is influenced by the society and culture in which we find ourselves and so we must avoid the pretence that our own preferred understanding is inherently superior, whereas in fact it will have its own characteristic prejudices, just like any other. In other words, we must never lose sight of the fact that we divide the world up differently when our interests are different, or if certain aspects about the way we are situated in that world or perceive that world change. The same goes for understanding the way in which our ideas change: if certain aspects of our own epistemological and ontological assumptions were different then we might not use the same concepts.

In developing his own interpretation of leisure in a way that corresponds to the one we began with in this book in Chapter 1, Karl Spracklen (2009: 13–17), in *The Meaning and Purpose of Leisure*, asserts that 'there are three ontologies of leisure': leisure as it is defined by freedom of choice in opposition to other areas of our lives that are more structured, e.g. work, education; 'leisure as structurally-constrained choice (or no choice)'; and leisure as 'completely free choice' in a world in which the structures that have hitherto historically restricted freedom of choice are breaking down, e.g. social class, gender and racial inequality. In developing his analysis Spracklen thereafter situates these 'ontologies' directly in relation to three corresponding 'epistemologies' of critical studies of leisure, which he locates in the historical and intellectual development of leisure studies: first, the optimistic conception of leisure as freedom associated with liberal theories; and second, structuralist theories of leisure which lay emphasis on the illusion of leisure as an autonomous liberatory domain and its role as a key reproducer existing social inequalities (the two most obvious examples of these are Marxism, which identifies the ways in which leisure is structuring and structured of social class relations, and feminism which emphasizes the ways leisure perpetuates patriarchal inequalities); and finally, postmodern theories which stress the very impossibility of structure – the manifestation of leisure is in fact marked by the absence of any structural presence.

Notwithstanding the incorrectness of Spracklen's use of the terms ontology and epistemology – to use them in the plural is a misnomer: ontology is theory of what exists, not theories of what exists and epistemology is theory of knowledge, not theories of knowledge – his argument is also limited by its understanding of freedom. Spracklen either fails to recognize that freedom is *always* a social relation (Bauman, 1988) – it can't be anything else because as human beings we are all the time situated in the world in some social setting, in some culture, and in some time and place. Or, he is setting postmodernism up as a straw target. Either, way, what he fails to make clear is that when we as leisure scholars talk about leisure we are always guided by how we as individuals are situated in the world, which not only determines our own epistemological and ontological assumptions, but also crucially informs our own ideological perspective. This line of reasoning not only renders Spracklen's third 'ontology' of leisure as 'completely free choice' invalid, but highlights the limits of the understanding of postmodernism and postmodernity in leisure studies. I will return to this second issue in Chapter 5. For the moment it is important to consider in more specific detail the strengths and weaknesses of structural theories of leisure as well as the epistemological and ontological assumptions that underpin them since, as we saw in the discussion developed in Chapter 1, they are markedly at odds with the optimistic conception of leisure as freedom associated with liberal theories.

In the limited space we have in this chapter it will be necessary to concentrate on only three interlacing aspects of structural constraint and their associated theoretical perspectives: social class, gender and racism. If these three approaches have anything in common, it is that they all have their roots in eighteenth- and nineteenth-century rational empiricism and the similar ideas of the 'founding fathers' of sociology which, as I subsequently argue, no longer constitute an overarching narrative of sufficient power, simplicity and wide appeal to compete with the recent changes in modernity, which means that they are getting further and further removed from the social reality in which contemporary leisure is experienced.

SOCIAL CLASS AND LEISURE

As we saw in the last chapter, historians' tenacious insistence on using the idea of social class as a central organizing concept has 'shown in a variety of ways the significance of leisure in the formation of class cultures and the mediation of their relationships, culturally and ideologically' (Bailey, 1989: 122). Like the idea of leisure itself, however, social class is also reflective of the double hermeneutic, namely the measure of the idea as it is used in academic discussion in leisure studies and by ordinary men and women in everyday language, and as a result, just as it implies different phenomena when employed in different theoretical traditions, it also means different things to different people.

The theoretical tradition that Marxists work with assumes that people's motivations, values and beliefs are derivative of their social class position and their material interests. In a nutshell, the material economic base determines the superstructure of society's intuitions and society itself is characterized by exploitation and a social class struggle arising from the means of production, which results in major inequalities in life chances, such as in education, housing health, job security, which all impact on our leisure opportunities. Marxism's great theme in all its versions is one about the possibility of 'man' overcoming his four-fold alienation – from himself, from his fellow-man, from his work and his products – and gaining his freedom through equality in a future communist society which will once and for all put an end to 'pre-history' and allow 'real history' to begin (Heller, 1999: 8). Unsurprisingly, Marxist inspired leisure studies also work with the assumption that leisure which is on offer in capitalist societies is alienating because capitalism makes real choice impossible. In this sense, capitalism also shapes our leisure (Clarke and Critcher, 1985). Writing from a neo-Marxist perspective, Herbert Marcuse, for example, describes leisure activity-experience as a requirement of capitalism 'to promote consumerism and the inculcation of false needs and wants, of ever new desires, so we will keep working for the money to buy more, rather than stop working in order that we may do more. The result, for Marcuse, is that leisure (and work) remain alienated because they are restricted, through consumer culture, to false necessity' (Slater, 1998: 400).

Neo-Marxist accounts suggest that sport in capitalist societies operates similarly. It is described as either a spectacle (Debord, 1967) or opiate (Brohm, 1978) which serves the double function of on the one hand diverting our attention away from more pressing political issues surrounding our alienation, while at the same time reducing the body to an instrumental means to an end – a virtual machine set with the task of maximizing capitalist production. The result of this is that the body ceases to be a source of pleasure and fulfilment in itself. Instead pleasure and fulfilment depend on what is accomplished with the body and satisfaction comes in terms of competitive outcomes rather than the physical experience of involvement. This view echoes with the concepts developed in the more generalized critical theory offered by Morgan (1994) in his *Leftist Theories of Sport* which argues that the institutionalization of sport ultimately corrupts. Morgan argues that the market norm, which is underpinned by the competitive pursuit of financial reward, undermines the intrinsic value of sports participation and the upshot of this is that athletes can be expected to cheat and break rules since it is commercial gain not sport itself which is all important (Blackshaw and Crabbe, 2004).

The work of Adorno and Horkheimer (1944), two of the most perceptive Marxist philosophers of modern times, perhaps best of all sums up the neo-Marxist perspective of leisure. They argue that it is not possible to separate human consciousness from the material existence of people's lived condition. To understand leisure, their works suggest, all we need to do is look at the chaotic existence of the global world we inhabit today, which originated in the USA, where a religion of serial consumption was established along with the idea that continuing acquisition of ever bet-ter-looking, better-performing material goods makes life perfect, which is mediated through the filter of the 'culture industry'. This is Adorno and Horkheimer's metaphor for popular culture which in their view pro-duces standardized leisure goods that render us merely passive consumers, exploited in our leisure time just as we are in the workplace. As they state:

> The man with leisure has to accept what the culture industry manufactur-ers offer him. Kant's formalism still expected a contribution from the indi-vidual, who was thought to relate the varied experienced of the senses to fundamental concepts; but industry robs the individual of this function. Its prime service to the customer is to do his schematizing for him
>
> (pp. 8–9)
>
> ... .The might of industrial society is lodged in men's minds. The enter-tainments manufacturers know that their products will be consumed with alertness even when the customer is distraught, for each of them is a model of the huge economic machinery which has always sustained the masses, whether at work or at leisure – which is akin to work
>
> (p. 13).

The theory of the leisure class

Veblen's (originally published in 1899) influential reading of the conspicu-ous consumption associated with those social elites – aristocracy, *bourgeois*, *nouveaux riches* – who perceived that their enjoyment of leisure was what distinguished them from the rest of society is obviously a precursor of Adorno and Horkheimer's neo-Marxist approach. In Veblen's view, con-spicuous consumption was above all else instrumental (Bauman, in Rojek, 2004): to be in a position not to have to do paid work was to be almost a 'gentleman'. As Bauman points out, it was a way of telling your 'signifi-cant others' (those also selectively admitted to the leisure class) just how high up the social hierarchy you had managed to climb, and that you had the means of settling there for good. Herein it was the display and exhibi-tion of your ability to consume conspicuously that was important, not the consumption *per se*. The novelty of consuming was no doubt important to the leisure class, but their aspirations for social prestige guaranteed that it was a virtue that they should contain their passions; the consumer goods and experiences accumulated were, as Bauman suggests, valued as posses-sions first and all the rest after.

In his work on postmodernity Bauman presents an equally uncom-promising assessment of the 'new leisure class': the celebrities (and those who service and profit from the electronic circus of celebrity culture) whose *raison d'être* is also to conspicuously consume, but as well to be conspicuously consumed by others. As Bauman (p. 294) makes clear, though, the consumption by and of this new 'leisure class' is not instrumental: 'it is "autotelic", a value in its own right, pursued for its own sake; it is its instrumental functions that have now turned instrumental and are no longer allowed to override or even to push into the second place its erstwhile pleasure-giving task'. As he asserts:

> Celebrities may come from the world of politics, of sport, of science or show business, or just be celebrated information specialists. Wherever they come from, though, all displayed celebrities put on display the world of celebrities – a world whose main distinctive feature is precisely the quality of being watched – by many, and in all corners of the globe: of being global in their capacity of being watched.
>
> (Bauman, 1998: 53)

To paraphrase what Adorno and Horkheimer (1944: 12) said about the movies, what Bauman is suggesting here is that 'real' life is becoming indistinguishable from the world of celebrity. Celebrity culture, far surpassing its own theatre of illusion, leaves no room for imagination or reflection on the part of its eager audience, who is unable to respond with the structure of world in which celebrity is the pinnacle of social achievement, yet deviate from its precise detail without losing the thread of its larger than life soap opera – anything from divorces to deaths of princesses; hence celebrity forces its 'victims' to equate it directly with reality. As we saw in Chapter 1, however, individuals in their roles as consumers are not so much brainwashed by ideology as lacking the appetite for the class struggle and ideologies are relegated to the background, while a hegemonic embrace of capitalism discloses a sense of what is really at stake: a consumer existence versus an authentic life.

Bourdieu: *habitus*, field and capital

Like Adorno and Horkheimer, the French sociologist Pierre Bourdieu is critical of the economic determinism found in the more unsophisticated versions of Marxist analyses of leisure and his thinking requires that we move towards a more general theory of consumerism that nonetheless retains the significance of economic capital. In this sense, Bourdieu's social theory of 'distinction' is an explicit attempt to understand the nature of social class and social class divisions in a complex world in which production has largely given way to consumption. Accordingly, he offers what is essentially a treatise on taste. For Bourdieu (1984) social class, like gender and 'race', needs to be understood as much by its *perceived* existence as through its *material* existence in the classical Marxist sense. To make this synthesis he draws on a theoretical toolkit featuring the concepts of field, *habitus* and capital.

Fields reflect the various social, cultural, economic and political arenas of life, which form their own microcosms of power endowed with their own rules. Leisure is structured in this way. Power struggles emerge in leisure fields as a result of the belief of social actors that the capital(s) of the field are worth fighting for. To draw on one example, the question is not just whether Italian opera is superior to Chinese opera, but also 'the series of institutions, rules, rituals, conventions, categories, designations, appointments and titles', which constitute the objective hierarchy of opera, 'and which produce certain discourses and activities' (Webb *et al.*, 2002: 21–2). Analogous to fluctuations in the stock market, the 'currency' or rates of exchange attached to particular capitals in particular fields are also vulnerable to change as these are continually contested.

In order to synthesize the relationship between the individual and society, or more precisely, his or her relationship with a highly differentiated consumer world constituted by these fields of power, Bourdieu draws on Marcel Mauss's use of the concept of *habitus*. Bourdieu (2000) suggests that the *habitus* is an embodied internalised schema which is both structured by and structuring of social actors' practices, attitudes, and dispositions. The *habitus* also constitutes and is constituted by social actors' practical sense of knowing the world and it is through their 'feel for the game' of the leisure field in question – in our example the world opera – that they come to see that world and the position of themselves and others in that world as unexceptional. Vital to understanding this 'perfect coincidence' is the idea of the social actor's *doxa* values or 'doxic relation' to that field and world, which Bourdieu identifies with that tacitly cognitive and practical sense of knowing of what can and cannot be reasonably achieved. In this sense, the *habitus* constitutes only an 'assumed world' captured as it is through the confines of the individual social actor's 'horizon of possibilities' (Lane, 2000: 194).

In leisure, the practices, attitudes, and dispositions which social actors both adopt and embody ultimately depends on the extent to which they can position themselves in any given field and their particular 'endow-ment of capital'. For Bourdieu, capital

> is any resource effective in a given social arena that enables one to appropri-ate the specific profits arising out of participation and contest in it. Capital comes in three principal species: economic (material and financial assets), cultural (scarce symbolic goods, skills, and titles), and social (resources accrued by virtue of membership in a group). A fourth species, symbolic capital, designates the effects of any form of capital when people do not per-ceive them as such ... The position of any individual, group, or institution, in social space may thus be charted by two coordinates, the *overall volume and the composition of the capital* they detain.
>
> (Wacquant, 1998: 221)

What this suggests is that 'the profits of membership' offered by leisure are not available to everybody in the same way. This is because, as Ball (2003:4) asserts, the point of all 'capitals' is that they are resources to be *exploited* and it is their exclusivity in the battle for distinction that gives them their value. In other words, people who realize their own capital through their leisure interests do so specifically because others are excluded.

According to Bourdieu, social capital, like cultural capital, has two deci-sive features: on the one hand, it is a tangible resource made by advantage of social networks, and on the other, it has a symbolic dimension, which contrives to hide networks of power woven into the fibres of familiar-ity. In the event, Bourdieu's understanding of capital suggests that it is related to the extent, quality and quantity of social actors' networks *and* their ability to mobilize these, which is always governed by the mutual understanding that any given leisure field is an arena of struggle and it is the battle for distinction that gives capital its qualities. The upshot of this 'battle for distinction' is that it ends up symbolically approving the leisure interests of the most powerful, e.g. opera, ballet, classical music, etc. and disapproving those of the weakest groups, e.g. shopping, sport, pop music, etc. What this tells us is that the world of leisure is made up of different sites of symbolic rivalry. As Skeggs (2009) argues, the battle for distinction in leisure is also often accompanied with 'a gaze', or a 'look that could kill', that embodies a symbolic reading of who has and who hasn't the right to certain kinds of leisure, and which makes those who are perceived as unworthy feel 'out of place'. This is what Bourdieu calls symbolic violence.

As Blackshaw and Long (2005) argue, put directly in terms of leisure policy, symbolic violence has the larger effect of normalizing the marginality of the weakest groups who are treated as inferior and denied the kind of trust that they could manage public resources for themselves. This in turn not only limits their opportunities for social mobility, but also 'naturalizes' their inadequacy since how they see and experience the world is not taken into account. This delineation of the world, Bourdieu writes, works thus:

> Like a club founded on the active exclusion of undesirable people, the fashionable neighbourhood symbolically consecrates its inhabitants by allowing each one to partake of the capital accumulated by the inhabitants as a whole. Likewise, the stigmatised area symbolically degrades its inhabitants, who, in return, symbolically degrade it. Since they don't have all the cards necessary to participate in the various social games, the only thing they share is their common excommunication. Bringing together on a single site a population homogeneous in its dispossession strengthens that dispossession, notably with respect to culture and cultural practices: the pressures exerted at the level of class or school or in public life by the most disadvantaged or those furthest from a 'normal' existence pull everything down in a general levelling. They leave no escape other than flight toward other sites (which lack of resources usually renders impossible).
>
> (1999: 129)

In the event the most powerful groups in society maintain their positions in the social hierarchy not only with the aid of economic capital, but also the social and cultural capital embodied in their leisure life-styles: a combination of earning power and superior taste. On top of that, the most vulnerable groups tend to be blamed for their own misfortune since it is presumed they lack the right social and cultural resources to determine their own lives, which in turn encourages the superior 'us' to determine what is appropriate for the inferior 'them' (Blackshaw and Long, 2005).

From social class to leisure life-styles

Such has been Bourdieu's influence in leisure studies that in the mid-1980s some scholars began to argue that social class is becoming less significant to understanding leisure behaviour than individual life-style choices centred around patterns of consumption based on youth, gender and ethnicity. However, as Veal (2001) points out, there soon emerged a resistance to the use of the concept mainly based on the idea that leisure lifestyles may change but social classes and their identities remain essentially the same (as coal and diamond are essentially always carbon) (e.g. Critcher, 1989). However, such accounts tended to gloss the changed climatic conditions of advanced capitalism, finding it difficult to re-imagine 'workers' recast as 'consumers' – they merely saw workers consuming – who were increasingly able to occupy the place of consumption in new and imaginative ways through their leisure interests and activities.

During the 1990s the concept of leisure life-styles continued to grow in significance especially with more and more people rejecting lives made to the measure of social class, and even to some extent age, gender and ethnicity, for those which they perceived did not restrict other potential outlets for credulity. As I argue in *The Sage Dictionary of Leisure Studies* (2009), leisure life-styles today are thus seen from the perspective of leisure lifestyle theorists as more to do with the individual search for authenticity in a world where authenticity is an impossibility, for example, as we saw in the discussion of extreme leisure in Chapter 2. In this view, leisure lifestyles have little to do with other significant aspects of our sense of social self either, such as national identity, except during major international sports tournaments such as the association football or rugby union world cups. They are seen, rather, as identikits constructed and facilitated by global flows of consumer products and culture. The upshot is that rather than seeing leisure life-styles as being unable to provide the kinds of stable identities associated with social class or work, leisure scholars have to come to grips with the idea that a new kind of society has emerged. This is what some leisure scholars call postmodernity (see Rojek, 1995) in which there is an increasing recognition of the notion of the quick fix self-effacement and re-assembly, rather than some gradual shrinking, fading away, ultimately disappearing notion of fixity. In this view, the adoption of a new leisure life-style then – we must accept – is often nothing more (and nothing less either) than something more, hopefully, much more potentially exciting, empowering than the last one.

GENDER AND LEISURE

The first two things to note about the study of gender in leisure studies is that it is largely slanted towards women's leisure and there is not a wide range of different types of feminist leisure studies – and what there is, in Rojek's (2000: 112) view, produces 'a high degree of repetition in argument'. Indeed, contrary to what Spracklen (2009) and Green (1998) suggest, there are no 'radical feminist' researchers in leisure studies and postmodernity and poststructuralism are not becoming the 'new ortho-doxies' in feminist writings on leisure. The fundamental ideas underpin-ning feminist leisure studies all have their roots in second-wave feminism, although it has to be said that some researchers have drawn on basic insights from cultural studies, postmodernism and poststructuralism in order to show how they relate to the network of issues relating to social, economic, cultural and political injustice (Wearing, 1998; Aitchison, 2003).

The starting point of feminist leisure studies, like all other feminist research, is that the social organization of society is patriarchal, as well as capitalist, and as a result the constraints which limit women's leisure must be understood in terms of both these features. Three critical agendas lie at the heart of feminist leisure studies. It takes as its first agenda the criticism of the bias towards men's leisure in leisure policy and leisure studies. Its second agenda aims at identifying what is specific, central and important to women's leisure, while its third agenda is concerned with identifying alternative leisure opportunities supportive of women fulfilling their lei-sure potentials.

In developing these three agendas, feminist leisure studies exposes the tendency of 'malestream' leisure studies to overlook the ways in which the structural and everyday features of patriarchal capitalist societies combine to prevent women having the same individual choices, freedom and self-determination as men, and how this results in the structuration of their opportunities for leisure being for the most part circumscribed by their gender. If on the one hand leisure organization and bureaucracy devalues and limits women's leisure, on the other hand women find themselves in situations in which they find it difficult to express their individual agency. Feminists also reveal both the contingency and the multi-levelled ways in which women's leisure is constrained, not only directly due to the narrow range of activity options open to them, but also because of the tempo-ral, spatial, economic, ideological, socio-psychological factors involved, as well as the influence in this process of the categories of social class, 'race' and ethnicity and familial and other prescribed gender roles (see, for example, Deem, 1986).

A good example of this kind of research is Green *et al.*'s (1990) study of family, gender and leisure. Green *et al.* wanted to collect both general information about the types and levels of women's leisure participation as well as more detailed knowledge about women's perceptions and attitudes to leisure. The findings of their research confirmed that women's access to experiences of 'free-time' and leisure opportunities is structured by gender, social class, income level, age, ethnicity, work and domestic situation. They identified key constraints on women's leisure, such as time, money, non-availability of safe transport, childcare, number of children, and sexual orientation. They also found that the women most constrained were those not in paid employment, those with unemployed partners, lone parents and those married/living together with children. This study also showed that domestic work firmly remains women's work even if men help with it sometimes. Green, Hebron and Woodward's (1990) research suggests that a number of factors – social class, ethnicity, income, time and family – work alongside gender as pertinent factors in understanding women's leisure opportunities throughout the life course.

Another good example, which also enables us to explore the strengths and weaknesses of feminist leisure studies, is research that has been carried out into sexual exploitation in leisure. Sexual exploitation refers to the traumas caused by sex related physical abuse and emotional abuse and neglect. As I argue in *The Dictionary of Leisure Studies* (2009) though most leisure scholars are unanimous in their assertion that it is a serious problem in leisure, the actual ways in which they try to account for it differ in a number of key ways. One understandable response to the problem of sexual exploitation is extreme anger and offence. Such a standpoint is often reflected in media reports that scream out in the news seemingly every day, encompassing a blame culture that points to the incompetence of the government and the prison service for not dealing effectively enough with perverts and paedophiles. From this standpoint, sexual exploitation is often described as symptomatic of a more general moral malaise in society, though not always. Invariably the upshot is that perpetrators are held to be firmly responsible for their actions and there is an emphasis, on retribution against those who are usually adults in powerful positions, who are perceived to have failed usually young people. Solutions to the problem of sexual exploitation are more often than not seen in terms of harsher punishments and greater legal powers and controls over the perpetrators. The major problem with this approach is that in generating such levels of moral repugnance it leads to unreflective condemnation.

Feminist researchers have tended to adopt a rather different approach, seeing it as a technico-administrative problem to be solved rather than a *moral* issue, in the sense that their approach involves trying to separate the 'facts' from values. In other words they offer an approach to sexual exploitation that aims to eliminate subjective judgements in order to concentrate on the known 'facts' about the problem. This approach often involves studying the statistical distribution of abuse in particular leisure settings, or comparing a group of known abusers with a group of non-abusers, in order to identify and isolate the factors that make it more likely that some adults will abuse young people under their care.

For example, the feminist leisure scholar Celia Brackenridge (2001) has called sport 'the last bastion of child abuse,' estimating that as many as one in five young athletes may have experienced sexual victimization by adults overseeing their careers. Brackenridge says that there is still little research on sexual abuse in sport. For this reason, it is unclear which sports are most at risk, although she says abuse cases in the media tend to involve sports that require a high degree of intimacy between coach and athlete, including visits to the coach's home and shared accommodation. The stage just before peak performance, known as 'stage of imminent achievement' is a particularly critical period; sports at which this stage coincides with puberty are thought to pose the greatest risk of exploitation. Most cases, Brackenridge suggests, involve the power to reward and coerce and centre on an older male authority figure, who also has the expert and charismatic power to exploit dependent young female athletes.

In attempting to establish what she sees as a 'realistic' policy agenda Brackenridge (2001) acknowledges the dilemmas presented by contemporary theoretical deconstructions of gender for institutions that have been built on sex segregation. However, it is significant that discussions of 'how the dominant ideologies of "heterosexual masculinity" and "family" combine inside sporting subworlds to preserve male power and to stifle female autonomy' (p. 99) provide the *starting point* for the consideration of theory. Ultimately, whilst a contingency model of sexual exploitation is offered it is centred on the (positivist) assertion that 'sexual contact with an athlete is always wrong and always the responsibility of the coach or authority figure' (p. 240) whose judgements are a factor of the 'gender order of sport' (p. 238).

As Blackshaw and Crabbe (2004) point out, in many respects this understanding of sexual exploitation in sport can be related to wider populist concerns with rising levels of 'crime' and its material consequences which has evolved into what Downes and Rock (1998) refer to as a 'practical administrative criminology of the left', which has abandoned the search for 'causes' preferring to fall back upon the functionalist pursuit of social cohesion. Echoing Foucault's exploration of the implications for judging 'dangerous individuals' through expert knowledge, other recent analyses (e.g. Lianos with Douglas, 2000) have been equally concerned with the ways in which public perceptions have become more sensitized to danger and how the right to censure as a result of dangerization has come to feature more extensively in relation to crime control. They suggest that this 'new attitude to deviance is a side effect of new forms of social regulation' based on dangerization, which has seen society develop the tendency to perceive and analyse the world through categories of threat which invokes the tacit assumption that the world 'out there' is unsafe and that as a consequence it becomes essential to continuously scan and assess public and private spaces for potential threats, namely perverts and paedophiles.

As a result of these factors threats of danger are exaggerated – as are the identities of individuals perceived as threatening – to the extent that the probability of becoming a victim of a dangerous crime seems to be omnipresent. Nowhere is the ubiquitous probability of victimization felt more than in relation to the threat of sexual abuse by 'paedophiles' in sport. According to Brackenridge, sport faces two particular problems in relation to this threat. First, committed paedophiles use it as a way to get access to young people, and second, a culture has developed in sporting circles under which sexual liaison and banter is widely and sometimes inappropriately tolerated.

As Blackshaw and Crabbe's account suggests, as much as is possible, Brackenridge's technico-administrative approach to abuse in sport aims to eliminate the subjective and value judgements associated with paedophilia in order to concentrate on the known 'facts' about the problem in sport. However, the key problem with this approach is that it evidences an *essentialist* or *absolutist* view of sexual exploitation in which the problem of paedophilia is thus seen to be shaped by intrinsic, instinctual and overpowering forces in the individual that not only shape the personal but the social as well. The implication, leading from such assertions, is the answer to the problem of sexual exploitation lies in men's genes rather than in patriarchy and culture. From this perspective, then, it is biological and instinctual forces – which are basically male – that form the perversion for paedophilia. Consequently, the question of whether sexual exploitation is really an autonomous realm or 'natural' force which the 'social' controls is never really considered.

This approach to managing the risk of paedophilia in sport reflects what Feeley and Simon (1992) have described as the new penology, which is basically concerned with the efficient administration of risk and danger in contemporary societies. The problem is that this approach not only increases public perceptions about the probability of paedophiles operating in sport, but it also provides the general public with tangible targets of dangerousness that can be dealt with. Ultimately this technico-administrative approach ends up paying exclusive attention to coaches and the 'abused' at the expense of including the study of the 'experts' and others who are charged with the identification and protection of young people at 'risk' of 'danger' in their leisure. This does not mean that we should not consider important the influences which relate to abusers and abused, but it does suggest that the issue of how and why some individuals and not others come to be labelled as abused is also a problem in its own right.

RACISM AND LEISURE

To understand how inequality bears on leisure we must also consider the issue of racism. As I point out in *The Dictionary of Leisure Studies* (2009), this is the belief in the intrinsic superiority of one ethnic or cultural group over another and/or the perverse dislike or hatred of people from that group. In defining racism, a distinction also needs to be drawn between racialization, involving personalized acts of bigotry (which are often dependent on stereotypes about ethnic or cultural characteristics) levelled at other individuals because of their perceived difference, and structural racism involving societal institutions which support racial prejudice and discrimination. It needs to be recognized, therefore, that the opportunities for leisure afforded to ethnic minorities, such as Afro-Caribbean people and the different Asian groups, for example, are not simply a matter of the extent to which they are confronted by racism, but are also likely to be influenced by the patterns of prejudice and discrimination they have to face in other social formations, such as the labour market, housing, health, and all the rest besides, as well as the attendant forms of psychosocial, cultural, political and economic exclusion which accompany these. What this suggests is that the issue of racism in leisure cannot be divorced from social class and gender.

I also argue that in order to make sense of how racism arises in leisure, we must also not only recognize that human-being-in-the-world is a corporate undertaking in which people succeed in establishing distinctive ethnic cultures based on common values, but we must take into account the continuing legacy of colonialism, not only as a form of economic, social, political and judicial imperial rule, but as a cultural and intuitive one, too. The sport of cricket is a good example to draw on to illustrate both these pull and push processes. If, during the colonial period, cricket was an important part of an English model of sovereignty exported for making India governable to 'save it' from 'the political and religious despotism of native rule' (Rose 1999: 108), in a post-colonial world the same sport (along with the allure of Bollywood) has become the focal point for the sense of pride and national identity for what it means to be Indian – for rural farmers subsisting below the poverty line as well as for the new urban middle-class professionals thriving in the wake of the country's recent economic upturn. In this way, cricket has become the glue that holds together the imagined community (Anderson, 1991) of the Indian nation-state.

This example, notwithstanding, as John Spink (1994:17) points out, these two elements of internal ethnicity (pull) and external racism (push) are often difficult to separate, but what is clear is that time and again they can be seen operating together to maintain segregation between different ethnic groups in leisure. Indeed, if we look at popular leisure pursuits in Western countries, they are often marked with a 'very visible black cultural presence' (Harris, 2005: 226), but there is little evidence to suggest that these are representative of leisure more generally. Take for example, Stephenson and Hughes' (2005) research on race and tourism trends, which critically explores how black people's perceptions and experiences of tourism are influenced and structured by the social conditions of racialism and institutional racism. In particular, they explore how a penetrating and discriminating 'white gaze' (a racist governing form of surveillance), with racialist representations and stereotypes of black communities, societies and cultures, not only contributes to black people's disengagement from tourism, but even calls into question their explicit right to adopt a tourist identity.

It has also been demonstrated that even when a particular leisure activity or interest exhibits a highly visible ethnic minority presence, it can still be a site for perpetuating racist ideologies. For example, when exploring sports where there is a large Afro-Caribbean cultural presence, Hoberman (1997: 208) found that this is often used to reinforce stereotypes about black criminality by 'merging the black athlete and the black criminal into a single threatening figure ... first, by dramatizing two physically dynamic black male types which are often presumed to be both culturally and biologically deviant; and second, by putting the violent or otherwise deviant behaviour of black athletes on constant public display so as to reinforce the idea of the black male's characterological instability'.

Drawing on a similar research approach, Blackshaw and Crabbe (2005) consider the ways in which this kind of racism is both consumed and performed in sport, specifically in their research into the context of the mediagenic format of the courtroom trials involving the 'off-field' experiences of white and black players from professional football and rugby league. Building on Back *et al*'s (2001) important research in football, which leads them to assert that racialization is often contingent and ambivalent, as well as being articulated with other lines of social division, Blackshaw and Crabbe critically explore the ways in which the public performance, media representation and regulation of 'crime' are combined with racial and working-class stereotypes in order to reveal ostensible guilt.

Also focusing attention on the role of contingency and ambivalence in the way that the media perpetuate racism, I argue in Blackshaw (2008) that although anti-racism campaigns have done a great deal over the last 20 years or so to challenge racial discrimination in football, they have hitherto been poor at including football supporters as active participants through community action. Drawing on research findings gathered through participant observation at a Leeds United versus Blackburn Rovers match during the National Anti-Racism Week of Action in professional English football, I argue that campaigning tends to rely on managerial strategies which on the one hand draw on the vocabulary of community through the writing of a variety of media discourses and on the other stage-managed anti-racist spectacles in the hope that supporters will respond by repudiating racial discrimination and prejudice. I also argue that such strategies appear to be based on the idea that it is in the very heart of football's community – the stadiums – and the hope that the rhetorical effectiveness of media *persuasion* can be effectively combined with the spectacle of *manipulation* to challenge irrationalities of racism in the game.

However, this research shows that not only do these strategies have no large meaning for the majority of football supporters but also that in their culturally blinkered struggle for political correctness they may paradoxically perpetuate some of the very kinds of racism they are attempting to alleviate. Focusing, amongst other things, on the way in which *The Mighty Zulu Nation*, a young singing and dance group from South Africa, performed during the half-time interval to ostensibly introduce Zulu culture to the crowd, I argue that the spectacle of *manipulation* ultimately led to the day becoming nothing less than a staged portrayal of racialist stereotyping, albeit concocted and performed by 'authentic' Zulus. What this kind of research suggests, to paraphrase Back *et al.* (2001: 282), is that the legacy of racism in leisure is unfinished business, not least because of society's ability to combine old racism with new variants. What this last example tells us is that the phenomenon of racism in leisure today is much more complex than we once upon a time thought it was. What it also feasibly might suggest is that extant theories associated with understanding racism do not work as well as they once did.

REASSESSING SOCIOLOGICAL LEISURE STUDIES

This might lead us to speculate that social theory has lagged behind culture. In the next section I want to pursue this idea in some depth by looking at the work of Agnes Heller and Zygmunt Bauman, which taken together suggests that with their abiding faith in class and gender, in particular, as the central organizing ideas for understanding leisure, sociological leisure studies read increasingly like an eccentric curiosity in a vastly altered world.

There is a sentence, a paraphrasing of Nietzsche, which hangs over sociological leisure studies: 'I fear that we are not getting rid of class and gender because we still believe in grammar.' So deeply embedded are these modes of analysis in the *doxa* of sociological leisure studies they seem the natural place to look for anyone concerned with the complexity and defeat of inequality and injustice in leisure. The trouble with this cultural practice is that it does not work as well as it once did. The main reason for this, and the one that is most often overlooked, is the fact that the everyday leisure worlds of men and women – their inner and exterior lives and how these are individually experienced and shared with others – is one thing. Critical sociological discourse is quite another. There is always a slippage between the two and nowhere is this slippage today more conspicuous than with regard to the issue of how we understand leisure as a social phenomenon. In the last 30 or so years we have witnessed two revolutions: an economic revolution and what Agnes Heller (1998) calls the revolution of everyday life. So all-consuming have these two upheavals been that they have changed monumentally the ways in which most men and women see their places in the world. Moreover, with these changes the efficacy of class and gender as tools of analysis have deteriorated.

Let us look at these two revolutions in more detail. As we saw in the last chapter, with the advent of modernity the swinging pendulum of human destiny shifted decisively in favour of freedom over constraint. Moreover, at the same time a new form of social stratification based on industrial production and the essential prohibitions of class replaced feudalism and its closed system of stratification. This class-bound social order initially maintained extant patriarchal social relations until the mid-twentieth century. It is impossible to be precise about the why, the when, the where and the how of the revolution of everyday life, but, as historical studies show, Britain was still an austerity world until at least the 1950s, whose hardship and day-to-day drudge spoke of old certitudes and made most people feel old by the time they got to 50 (see Kynaston, 2007).

Most commentators locate the genesis of this revolution in everyday life in the changing social and cultural conditions of the 1960s (see Marwick, 1998). We are all familiar with the processes and events associated with this transformative decade which brought about improvements in material conditions and enabled the trend towards individualization and self-expression, which in turn led to the emergence of various social movements, youth culture and second-wave feminism that together challenged traditional conceptions of identity, youth, femininity and gender. But few leisure scholars have remarked on what this meant for human consciousness. Indeed, what is hardly ever acknowledged or commented upon is that at some point during this period the hitherto pervasive power of class was itself finally broken by the self-emancipation of *all* men and women.

What had seemed to be human destiny appeared overnight to turn itself into a gleeful dismantling of an orderly life to one of perpetual disembedding and reembedding, as Bauman puts it, drawing on the words of Giddens (Blackshaw, 2005). If modernity in its formative industrial production stage posed men and women dilemmas such as 'who am I?' and 'what am I to be?', these were now increasingly becoming a matter of self-awareness, self-definition and self-assertion (Bauman, 2008b), as opposed to being guided by unawareness, obligation and commitment, to a particular way of living that by now had become an object of irritation and a subject of caricature.

What Bauman is alluding to here is that by the second half of the twentieth century the foundering of old social solidarities and inequities forged through class and gender inequalities had opened the way for new freedoms and with these new opportunities for leisure. The world today is no longer that same one that led Richard Hoggart to observe that when 'people feel that they cannot do much about the main elements in their situation, feel it not necessary with despair or disappointment or resentment but simply a fact of life' (Hoggart, 1966: 92). It is now one in which we consider our lives are ours to pursue as *we* wish, within or even contrary to the constraints imposed by the world. What this also means is that the *habitus* into which we are born has less of a constraining influence on our lives (and our leisure lives) than would have been the case not so long ago.

Bauman knows of course that ours is far from being an equal society, that our lives are not completely free of their social class, gender or ethnic statuses, and that a democratic deficit continues to bedevil the leisure opportunities of some. However, it is an inescapable fact that the Western world is far less class-ridden (and sexist and racist) than it was a generation ago and that by now these previously 'solid' markers of identity and difference are much more fluid and permeable than they were in the not too distant past. One of the upshots of this is that most people no longer (if they ever did) perceive their leisure lives through the prisms of 'class' or 'gender'. Our lives today have a much more in-between, DIY readymade feel about them, and to this extent that they are better understood as *individualized* existences. A liquid modern life, in other words, has no solid ontological status, something that is given, is inevitable, we are predisposed to or firmly believe in. Some lives are no doubt more congealed than others, but anyone's *habitus* is just something that is until further notice. In other words, it seems to fit you as a person who chooses to live this kind of life rather than another.

As Bauman (1990) points out, human identity has in the process been transformed from a 'given' into a 'task', and for the first time in history it seems that everybody is in a position to think of themselves in ways that until recently in human history had only been the prerogative of the most affluent (and the abnormal): as individuals *de facto,* which means exceeding the possibilities of the limits of their class, gender, culture or family situation. With this great transcendence of consciousness Mark Two, Bauman's sociology suggests, modernity has transformed itself into a world where people, no matter what their status at birth, are increasingly refusing to accept the way they are 'supposed' to live, recognizing as they do that their lives are now about choice. With this revolution what the world seems to be saying to men and women today, who now imagine themselves as individuals first and foremost, is this: 'forget who you are and if you cannot be what you want to be, imagine that you can'. To be a modern man or woman today is to be an individual *de facto*, which also means to be free with all of individuality's loneliness, responsibility, existential angst, unavoidable desires, and so on, and in particular the readiness to take chances. In the words of Alexander Nehmas (1998) this means that today you are almost compelled to do something with your life 'that is both significant and very different from whatever has been done before'. It also means that you are charged with the task of ensuring that your own individual existence does not remain without a purpose.

A life lived as an individual *de facto* is what Heller describes as a contingency life, which is the opposite of the kind of life lived in the totality of a class system; men and women who inhabit a contingent world, one in which they are individuals who are wholly contingent, yet make out of that very circumstance their own identities, which they may or may not choose to share with others, become contingent beings by having been stripped of that kind of innocence. As Richard Rorty (2007) suggests, people who think of themselves as contingent know that who they are is merely a matter of contingency, i.e. due to the kind of family they are born into, the city in which they are born, and everything else besides. They are also consciously aware that things could always be different, that, for example, the identity (and leisure) that moves them today might be different tomorrow. In other words we are all in the position of the protagonist, Corporal Coetzee from South Africa, in J.M. Coetzee's (2009a) *'Summertime': 'Undated Fragments'*, who during the occupation of Italy by the Allied troops was one of those soldiers who had their 'recreations' put on for them via free performances in the big opera houses:

> Young men from America, Britain, and the far-flung British dominions across the seas, wholly innocent of Italian opera, were plunged into the drama of *Tosca* or *The Barber of Seville* or *Lucia di Lammermoor*. Only a handful took to it, [but he] was among that handful. Brought up on sentimental Irish and English ballads, he was entranced by the lush new music and overwhelmed by the spectacle. Day after day he went back for more ... So [that when he] returned to South Africa at the end of hostilities, it was with a newfound passion for opera. '*La donna è mobile*,' he would sing in the bath. '*Figaro here, Figaro there*,' he would sing, '*Figaro, Figaro, Feeegaro!*' He went out and bought a gramophone, their family's first; over and over again he would play a 78 rpm recording of Caruso singing 'Your tiny hand is frozen.' When long-playing records were invented he acquired a new and better gramophone, together with an album of Renata Tebaldi singing well-loved arias.

It is this contingency-awareness *more than anything else* that today gives modern life its weight. Indeed, the world of *cosmic contingency*, of chance and accident, and the wanting to seek out new adventures and risks: that is the terrain of contemporary modern human existence. As Heller (1999) points out, to have this kind of consciousness is not only to have grasped the point that your life doesn't serve any purpose higher than being lived, it is also to have *historical* contingency-awareness, or to be aware that not so long ago, each and every person was believed to serve a special purpose in the world. Most men and women who inhabited modernity in its formative stage saw no need to recognize any of this. Today that world is more or less extinct and contingency-consciousness is more or less a ubiquitous phenomenon.

In the last 20 years we have also witnessed a Mark Two economic revolution, which has seen the emergence of neo-liberalism, the political doctrine that developed in earnest from the close of what Hobsbawm (1995) calls the 'short twentieth century' (1914–91) onwards, involving the ostensible denial of ideology, the affirmation of entrepreneurship in the light of the opportunities arising from capitalism in the period of intensified globalization, and the substitution of the market state for the sovereign state. With neo-liberalism the ideology of market fundamentalism has become so pervasive that it seems that there is nothing left in the world that is not commodifiable. With this trend we have also seen the substitution of consumerism for production as the main (de)regulator of our lives. By now consumerism bombards us, every day, with images of things that we can and can't afford to pay for, and encourages us to want all of them. Rational men and women know that their economic survival depends on buying only what they can afford, but the availability of seemingly unlimited credit encourages them to live above their means. The contemporary world is in effect a sociality in which once upon a time social class-bound virtues have been subsumed by credit, which as Peter Conrad (2006) recently argued in the *Observer* is, 'so long as you pay your, bills, proof of moral standing, and the merchants who extend it express their own faith in your probity'.

As Bauman (1998; 2000a) has consistently argued, consumerism has by now replaced the work ethic as the backbone of the reward system in a sociality which is underpatterned rather than patterned, disorganized rather than ordered. Life resembles the board game Snakes and Ladders, where a shake of the dice can lead to either a rapid ascent or a quick downward slide. It is only the losers in this game of chance who are still controlled through the work ethic. To put it simply the market has redrawn the boundaries between social class divisions as a relationship between those who happily consume and those who cannot, despite their want of trying. Social control is barely noticeable, except for 'terror suspects' and the 'flawed consumers', incapable of fulfilling their designated social positions as 'consumers first, and all the rest after', and whose subordinate position prevents them from participating freely in what has become for the masses a dream world of consumerism (Blackshaw, 2005).

So why was it that when the world was saying to the men and women, 'forget your location in the class system, and even if you can't be what you want to be, imagine that you can', they were by and large only capable of re-thinking themselves as individualized consumers? Or, to put the question in a more metaphysical form, why did they move, as Eric Fromm used to say, from a state of 'being' to a state of 'having', or we might say from self-emancipation to self-marketing? The straightforward answer is that ubiquitous contingency-consciousness emerged at the same time when the majority of people – for the first time – could afford to consume items that were not necessary for survival. And given the fact that from the very beginning, consumerism has always been about transport, taking the consumer out of the penumbra of the present and into another world, its success in engaging men and women as consumers should come as no surprise.

What are the implications of these two Mark Two revolutions for leisure studies? First and foremost, I'd say trying to persuade anyone that people who choose to live their lives as contingency conscious consumers constitute a class (or gender) with its own consciousness, shared collective identity, have similar interests and should develop the kinds of formal organization that would allow it to advance the conditions of its way of life, is a fairy tale. This is not to say that collective organization is unimportant. Neither is it to say that social inequality and injustice are not still very real problems. But it is to recognize that, just like the production-based society of Ernest Gellner's (1964) 'industrial man', the consumer-based sociality that men and women today inhabit has its own ways of stratifying, which includes its own inbuilt neo-liberal drive to maintain social hierarchies (including those paddings of privilege and stereotypes left over from feudalism and the social class society) and that these are made to the measure of consumerism, which means that they are couched in the language of diversity rather than equality and in the leisure sphere in terms of judgements of taste and the juxtaposing of different life-styles. All men and women living today know this; they also know that they are compelled *individually* to respond to the situation in which they find themselves in this consumer stratocracy.

Heller (1998) argues that there are actually three types of revolution: everyday life, economic and political. As we have seen the revolution of everyday life has resulted in self-emancipation and economic revolution has resulted in market fundamentalism. In simple terms, you could say that the one plus the other equals a new world that still awaits liberation through political revolution. As I see it, the major challenge facing leisure studies is the same one facing politics: how to link the revolution of everyday life to a Mark Two programme of political revolution in order to liberate men and women from market fundamentalism and consumerism. In any kind of politics the ability to tell convincing stories is the difference between success and failure. As I pointed out in the introduction to this book, metaphors are important to telling stories not only because they use language in magical and enlivening ways, but also because they are edifying and enlightening. But when metaphors fail to cast a spell, people do not listen to them.

Class in particular is a metaphor whose magic still burns brightly for many in critical sociological leisure studies but it is by now too faded to resonate with the lives of the majority of people today, who do not experience the world in the way that people of a class society did. As Heller (1998) points out, the upshot of this is that class no longer has any emancipatory force, which means that Marx's distinction between the idea of a 'class in itself' and a 'class for itself' does not carry any great weight – if it ever did. It is simply the case that the grammar of class does not have within its grasp an overarching narrative of sufficient power, simplicity and wide appeal to compete with individualization.

The most important challenge facing sociological leisure studies today, then, is how to overcome its estrangement from the everyday worlds of men and women and recognize that it is not class (or gender), but *individualization* that is today *the* shaping force in the narrative of human existence, and that *all* men and women are contingent people living contingent lives, and they are aware of their contingency. They have no secure destiny of any kind. To pretend that they still have is futile. From now on it will *always* be like this.

CONCLUSION

The first part of this chapter looked the relationships between social class, gender and ethnicity and leisure, while the second part reassessed leisure as a social phenomenon by discussing the implications for the study of leisure in the light of some profound social, cultural, economic and political changes which have developed in earnest since the closing decades of what Hobsbawm (1995) calls the 'short twentieth century'. The following conclusions may be drawn from this discussion. Although sociological leisure studies have customarily been a fruitful source for understanding inequalities in leisure, how people experience and understand leisure today can no longer be understood as simply 'classed', 'gendered' or 'raced'. The major task facing sociological leisure studies is how to re-acquaint itself with the habit of acquiring new metaphors made to the measure of lives that are individualized, decentred, episodic, fragmented, consumerist, sometimes magical, but always subject to uncertainty, anxiety, indecision and change. In other words, what sociological leisure studies need are new research agendas and ways of conveying the world that better reflect the lives of men and women today, which in the process restore agency to social actors by granting them the freedom to express and define the world in which *they* live and leisure. In the next chapter we shall pursue this challenge by examining in detail the idea of the postmodern imagination and the way in which it helps us to come to terms with this more complex modernity.

5

LEISURE IN THE POSTMODERN IMAGINATION

The difficulty in applying the idea of the postmodern imagination to leisure is that everyone seems to know exactly what to think. If we ask any reasonably well-read leisure studies scholar about the idea, we will learn that it went from being a revolutionary practice to an art form, from an art form to a new sensibility in leisure studies some time in the early 1990s, from a sensibility to a domesticated academic perspective, or just another 'ism', and finally became a form of contempt. If 'postmodernism' began as a programme of disruption in leisure studies, so the story goes, it is today a way of thinking that is largely derided.

While all this may be comforting to leisure studies, it is hardly accurate. No idea as contested as the postmodern imagination can be so neatly fitted into such a tidy compartment and thereafter be written off. What the postmodern imagination teaches us above all else is to recognize the *contingency* of culture. That is, whilst there are many ways of being-in-the-world, all humans share the meaning of what it means to be human – in other words all human beings have the sense of an inevitable, universal relation, but with contingency attached to the cultural form it will take. It is this key insight of the convergence of the contingent and the inevitable that alerts us to the ambivalence of human being-in-the-world. In accepting the contingency of the present, the postmodern imagination teaches us, we accept the 'untidy' ambivalence of life as it is lived by ordinary men and women. Not to do so is to leave ourselves open to the dangers of either cultural relativism or fundamentalism, which loom large whenever one of these two tendencies is reduced to the other. What the postmodern imagination teaches us first and foremost, to paraphrase Agnes Heller (2005: 23), is that contingency and inevitability if joined together can offer (perhaps) spaces in which they can coexist in tension. This is not a goal to be achieved, however, but a practice to be kept alive through hermeneutics.

At this point these observations might seem puzzling, but the postmodern imagination becomes more, rather than less, puzzling the better we come to understand it. There must be reasons for such an incongruity. Foremost among these, and as we saw in the last chapter, is the problem that leisure studies teaches us to look at the world from different perspectives, such as Marxism and class and feminism and gender, which to all intents and purposes resemble what the French philosopher Jean-François Lyotard (1984) calls grand narratives. What this chapter aims to demonstrate is that the postmodern imagination offers leisure studies a fresh way of thinking about the world. This is a way of thinking that does not depend on grand theory, but rather on metaphor, which is the rhetorical tool that enables us to 'defamiliarize the familiar' and show it in a new light (Bauman, 1990). In other words metaphor is that part of language that enables us to practice hermeneutics. That is, on the one hand, to make meaning, i.e. make intelligible that which could not otherwise be grasped, and on the other, to deepen our understanding so as to make meaning even more meaningful, in the process creating some democratic operating principles as we go along. Seen in this way, the postmodern imagination is the continuation of *skholē* by an alternative means, which retrains the educated imagination into looking for the hidden nuances, distortions, contradictions, contingencies, in other words, the ambivalence of what we casually call 'reality', and to see significance and meaning in unexpected places. Most leisure studies scholars resist this critical revisionism, while one or two notable exceptions have submitted themselves to the process with a marked improvement to their work. This is because in the postmodern imagination they recognize that there are certain intrinsic features which permit us to see leisure in a new light, and crucially, in a way that reflects how we experience it today.

As we have seen already, Chris Rojek has made a number of valuable contributions to leisure studies, but of all of his work it is his interest in the puzzle of 'postmodernism', which came to the forefront in leisure studies in the late-1980s, that provides his most telling contribution to the discipline. Here was a dramatic irony, by the mid-1990s 'postmodernism' had lost its magnesium flare fame, but at the very moment some were gleefully driving a stake through its heart, Rojek was using the postmodern imagination to give leisure studies a blood transfusion in his book *Decentring Leisure*.

DECENTRING LEISURE

As its title suggests, in this book, Rojek examines a concept integrally related to the postmodern imagination, the notion of 'decentring'. This is a book distinguished by its bibliographical comprehensiveness, which is reflected in the ambition of its exposition. Rojek not only assembles most of his arguments out of primary sociological sources, but he also provides the reader with an overview of the most significant interpretations from, and applied crucially, to leisure studies. His account thus reveals a full range of ideas relating to postmodern leisure.

Rojek's primary thesis is that there has been a radical shift in the study of leisure in the light of 'postmodernism', which questions the entire basis of the subject. This idea of 'decentring' leisure is ambivalent in the sense that it not only assumes that leisure studies is a discursive formation that exists independently of individual leisure scholars, but also that it should go about its day-to-day business by undermining the significance of its own unifying centre (the topic of leisure). In this sense Rojek is suggesting that although leisure studies cannot help but be perspectival, it must always strive to remain open to various other culturally determined ways of seeing the world. In other words, the modernist object of leisure 'as a bounded category of practice and experience' (Rojek, 1995: 146) needs to be subsumed into the subject of culture.

The first thing to say about *Decentring Leisure* is that it aims to provide a critical analysis of leisure in postmodernity, which at its most basic refers to a historical period subsequent to modernity. With the idea of postmodernity there is the assumption that one phase of modernity has more or less ended and another, however ill understood, has begun, which is accompanied by a distinct self-awareness of its own contingency. In this sense postmodernity needs to be understood as modernity 'coming to terms with its own impossibility; a self-monitoring modernity, one that consciously discards what it was once unconsciously doing' (Bauman, 1991: 272).

This is different to 'postmodernism', which for some commentators is a negative term that has been used to describe the wave of self-conscious novelty and experimentation and developments in fashion, social attitudes and culture that began to emerge with the period the historian Arthur Marwick (1998) called the 'long sixties', when radicals in fields as diverse as architecture, historiography and philosophy were creating their own styles of intellectual exposition, and not only that, but using them to dismember some of the putative ideals which had prevailed in their disciplines since the Enlightenment, which as we saw in Chapter 3 marked the age of modern reason bound to the twin ideas of rational inquiry and scientific method which emerged in the seventeenth century. What came to be called 'post-modernism' seemed to be transforming these 'modern' disciplines into something radically different by on the one hand moving them away from science and more closely to art and on the other breaking down assumed barriers between 'higher' and 'lower' forms of culture by paying keen attention to the quotidian of new and alternative socio-cultural developments, while at the same time celebrating their plurality in the process.

With the dissipation of the distinction between high and low culture, there emerged the assumption that the study of leisure could also be about taking things that previously were not considered worthy of concern – or even beneath contempt – and putting them centre stage in leisure studies. What Rojek draws from this is the idea that with these changes human-kind had finally crossed the line from innocence to knowledge and from now on it would always be like this. As we have seen already, his awareness of these cultural changes led him to argue that in order to really know how people *experience* leisure we must decentre the subject of leisure itself, but what it also told him was that there is nothing about the world that is quite what it seems and the way that we understand leisure should run in channels that are shallow as well as deep. This was essentially a critical response to 'modernist' leisure studies that had hitherto evinced a tendency to sacrifice surface to depth in the hope of revealing the innermost truths about our leisure experiences.

As commentators such as Fredric Jameson (1991) have observed, the urge to playfulness and pastiche is part and parcel of the postmodern outlook. Reality, invention and all kinds of cultural borrowings are playfully intertwined. Critical analysis is like leisure, which is also like art: not about representing things, it is about acting things out. In other words, leisure is performatively playful, which implies that life itself might be interpreted as a work of art. Yet there is little to be gained from individuals' life and their art because they are constantly staging both; postmodern men and women merely select the details of the world that interest them and make them decorative. Jameson argues that with 'postmodernism', the ability to live an authentic, freely chosen existence effectively disappears and is replaced by the almost universal practice of pastiche. In other words, mimesis becomes a universal practice, but with an ironic twist.

According to Umberto Eco, one of the upshots of this postmodernizing trend is that we develop an aesthetic approach to life with which there are no social judgements that are untouched by irony. In his view the postmodernist attitude is

> that of a man who loves a very cultivated woman and knows he cannot say to her "I love you madly" because he knows that she knows (and that she knows he knows) that these words have already been written by Barbara Cartland. Still, there is a solution. He can say, 'As Barbara Cartland would put it, "I love you madly"'

> (quoted in French, 2006).

As we have already seen, Lyotard (1984) has argued that the postmodern attitude is also marked by an 'incredulity towards metanarratives'. In other words, the collapse, in our time, of the illusions (including love) that gave energy to the Enlightenment and the modern imagination and modern systems of thought – whether Marxism, feminism, or any other kind of 'ism' – which are futile or comedic, depending which way you look at them. The arrival of negative 'postmodernism', so the argument goes, signals an age when any kind of certainty is suspect, when cynicism has become the key signifier of cool. At the heart of negative 'postmodernism' is the idea that the moral universe is no longer stable, that the areas of agreement about values and ethics have disappeared. There is no such thing as objective truth, which is a bad faith we would be better off without. Paroxysm and entropy are postmodernity's defining features, poised on the brink of dissolving into incoherence and coolness and indifference.

Critics have also argued that the arrival of 'postmodernism' has led to a world that is a depthless, hyperized asociality, where individual agency is irrelevant and which gives priority to the 'code' over subjective ideas and in the process marks the victory of the 'anti-social sign over the social sign' (Harland, 1987). It signals a paranoid, anomic world where renegades from the consumer society create their own paroxysm while a corrupt, capitalist state seeks to control and exploit both conformists and nonconformists alike – postmodern life is thus a hell of inauthenticity and what it lacks is the texture of a felt life. In other words, the world of 'postmodernism' is simply the outrider of a vast marketing strategy, a place where leisure is 'any consumption of unproductive time' (Baudrillard, 1981: 76). Human lives no longer proceed through a gradual cycling of ripening and rot. The hyper capitalist economy attempts to abolish adulthood altogether. Leisure – if we can be bothered with it or can afford it – merely enables us to keep fit in order to postpone the ageing process. In this way, leisure becomes

> irrevocably an *activity*, an *obligatory* social phenomenon. Time is not in this instance 'free' ... the individual is not free to escape it. No one needs leisure, but everyone is called upon to provide evidence of his availability for *unproductive* labour.
>
> (Baudrillard quoted in Rojek, 1990: 9)

Is it not ironic that in a world so lacking in originality and dramatic finesse leisure should be so seeped in commercial calculation?

There are echoes of all these ideas in *Decentring Leisure*, but Rojek astutely kneads them together and crumbles in some more rational insights. The book is divided into three parts, organized in broadly sequential fashion: Capitalism and Leisure; Modernity and Leisure; and 'Postmodernism' and Leisure. Here Rojek is concerned with the question, 'What is leisure in (post)modernity?' But he is specifically interested in how we *experience* leisure. Indeed, this is the issue to which he continually returns in all his work on leisure studies. In order to explore this question in *Decentring Leisure*, he identifies three social formations: capitalism, modernity and postmodernity.

Capitalism, modernity and postmodernity and leisure

As we saw in Chapter 3, the idea of modernity, or I should say, modernization, refers to the emergence of a new faith in the processes of scientific knowledge and technological advance which marks the beginning of modernity's separation from traditional society. It is against the background of postmodernity's separation from modernity that the current 'decentring' of leisure should be seen. We also saw in this chapter that capitalism is key to historical understandings of the emergence of modern leisure. Rojek suggests that there are absolutely two points to be made about capitalism: whereas for Marx it must be understood in terms of class relationships where the work process itself becomes wholly rationalized, but for Weber the engine of capitalism is the rationaliza-tion process itself. Under capitalism, which commodifies everything and leads to the rationalization of institutions and the 'disenchantment' of the world, Rojek argues, leisure is characterized by a deficit of meaning and a loss of its former intrinsic value. Capitalism is a market world of commodification and homogenization of experience from which there is little chance of escape.

This leads Rojek to make two crucial observations about leisure in modernity: if on the one hand it signifies rationality, order and social con-trol, on the other it is nothing more (and nothing less either) than a way of fulfilling consumers' empty time. This sense of ambivalence is summed up perfectly by Peter Bramham in his cogent review of Rojek's book:

> If modernity 1 was all about order, rationality and recreation, modernity 2 was about change, irrationality and pleasure. Rojek captures these disintegrat-ing, destructuring processes of modernity 2 by summarizing Nietzsche's four propositions about modernity. First, the rational order of modernity is an illusion; secondly, change is inevitable; thirdly, change must be posi-tively embraced and affirmed; finally, modernity 2 demands a celebration of unavoidable divisions and fragmentations. Leisure under modernity 1 was purposive and rational, for example, character-building outdoor pursuits offered hygienic and healthy countryside recreation. In modernity 2, leisure becomes postmodern shopping, promenading *flâneurie* – browsing, wan-dering, watching, wishing, and opening oneself up to the sensations and rhythms of the city.
>
> (Bramham, 2002: 230)

The 'official' message of Modernity 1 was 'solidly' modern: progress, order and self-improvement; the 'unofficial' message of Modernity 2 is just the opposite. In developing his thesis Rojek compares these key aspects of Modernity 2 to what he sees as characteristic aspects of post-modernity, which include the following: ambivalence, individualization, the idea of the self and private devotion, rationality, secularism, capi-talism, consumption, globalization, irony, curiosity and intellectualism. Wherever there are intimations of postmodernity, Rojek identifies a pre-cursor in modernity. For example, the roots of postmodern rootlessness can be found in modernity. This is a world of contradictions, grand and provincial, classifying and chaotic, prosaic and poetic, where men and women feel at home in their allotted social class identities, but also utterly hemmed in.

Rojek's tacit assumptions about this link become explicit in .ding discussion of modernity and leisure, when he argues that ungs are without doubt: First, 'Modernity 1's attempt to arrange ial differentiation of society generated irresistible de-differentiat-, tendencies' (Rojek, 1995: 101). For example, the gap between what we understand as work on the one hand and leisure on the other is often contradictory: work and leisure appear not to talk to each other, yet are in constant communication; they seem to have little in common, yet often have much in common. Second, analysing leisure only in 'evolutionary terms', as historians typically do, is insufficient, since just as leisure is likely 'centred' in modern experience and distinctive in form, it is just as likely to be 'decentred' and formless. Third, the precarization tendencies emanating from differentiation and de-differentiation challenge leisure scholars to place people's *experience* of leisure (rather than leisure as a thing in itself) at the centre of their analyses.

After providing a brief discussion of the phenomenology of leisure, which identifies the embodied character of our being-in-the-modern-world that significantly determines the ways in which we perceive and act in our leisure – restlessly, wantingly, nostalgically, poetically, searching for an authentic existence and something like a home in a world in which neither exist – Rojek proceeds to assess postmodern leisure. There is not the space here to deal with Rojek's own assessment of postmodernization. What I shall do instead is offer my own exposition, which is illustrated with both leisure examples and my own research in leisure studies.

POSTMODERNIZATION AND LEISURE

The modern social and economic conditions that brought with them a modern world in which the ideal bourgeois citizen was assumed to be cautious and apprehensive, content to defer gratification and paying the price of present pleasures forgone has been superseded by a postmodern sociality in which individualization dominates more than anything else. In sociology individualization has come to categorize the two phases of life, experience and perception reflected respectively in modernity and postmodernity. In Lash's (2002b) view, the major difference between modern and postmodern individualization is that the former is *reflective,* mirroring the underlying tensions between individual agency and the structural determinants of a modern society built on differences such as social class, gender, ethnicity and age. Leisure subcultures are good examples of the way in which reflective individualization works, especially in relation to particular style groups, such as the teddy boys, mods and skinheads, as they emerged respectively in the 1950s, 1960s and 1970s. With the emergence of postmodernity, however, individualization has become *reflexive*. As Lash points out, reflexes are indeterminate and immediate and as a consequence of liquid modern change reflexive individuals are those individuals who have to cope with living in an uncertain, speeded-up world, which demands quick decision-making. Michel Maffesoli's (1996) neo-tribes, otherwise known as the 'little masses' of the uncertain and fragmenting consumer society, are good examples of reflexive individualization in action.

The postmodern citizen unencumbered by his or her social class is not averse to throwing caution to the wind. S/he is on the contrary given to instant gratification, to putting off until further notice planning for future hardships, and unwilling to forgo pleasures. Self-transformation is not merely a possibility, but it is a duty to one's individuality, because in postmodernity the lived life is the only life worth living. Modernity's structures continue to fragment and its once upon a time central characters, defined by their social class, gender, ethnicity and age identities fade out of the narrative; there is no clear never-to-be-repeated life trajectory on offer any more, no obvious time-line, no arcs, no one best moment, only 'the end'. 'Maybe, this time, I could be somebody else' – that is the point of life, which is a contingency world where *everyone* is capable of transforming their identity. Underneath many of our leisure interests there is this same subconscious, which is palimpsest and naturally 'individualized' and 'private', rather than 'social' and 'communal'.

Bauman (1997) argues that postmodern lives are first and foremost guided by a 'will to happiness', which is progressively more individualized as social relationships are increasingly lifted out of their more traditional social class contexts to form new *habitats*, which 'unbind' time and weaken the coercive impact of the past. In a nutshell, with the onset of postmodernity, life has increasingly come to be experienced in *pointillist* time (Bauman, 2007), marked by ruptures and discontinuity; it is not linear but delivers innumerable co-existing fragments. Postmodern lives also exude a jumble of uncalculated lack of concern for sequentiality and, in some cases, consequentiality. Postmodern men and women are like the characters in Borges' world of Tlön, who feel that their everyday world, their past, and the past of their forebears, is always slipping away from them, as if they are drowning in a new, overwhelming sea of a world they cannot make out. It is not so much a deep sinking as a surface trawl – that's the thing about postmodern life: its vicissitudes are underpatterned rather than patterned, ephemeral rather than lasting, ultimately unfulfilling rather than satiating.

The upshot is that men and women are likely to look in two directions for guidance on how to live their lives: on the one hand towards the past whose shaping of them they have a duty to ludicly explore (even if this is a false nostalgia, or nostalgia for a life that wasn't lived) and, on the other, towards a present which they are constantly trying to keep up with. The past, like the present, seems up for grabs, available for playful reinvention. As Terry Eagleton (2005) has suggested, in postmodernity, our leisure experiences, once a silent mechanism for resisting the dominance of consumer culture, are now merely another 'species of it'. As he puts it:

> Instead of wandering along Hadrian's Wall, we have the Hadrian's Wall Experience: instead of the Giant's Causeway, the Giant's Causeway Experience. What we consume now is not objects but our sensations of them ... In an ultimate postmodern irony, a commodified experience compensates for the commodity's impoverishment of experience. The term 'experience' dwindles to an empty signifier.

If modernity was a world in which 'its world was *the* world', postmodernity 'is constructed in an inclusive fashion; all realities are accommodated as possibilities' (Ferguson, 2009: 180).

Postmodern men and women may claim that they are devoted to their various leisure pursuits, but in most cases it is a throwaway gesture, a means of giving nothing of themselves, and absorbed only for themselves. It turns out that postmoderns perhaps might not be very interested in leisure at all, only in the psychodrama of it. Leisure is just buzz, feeling, lots of cool, colour and crash, not so much a devotional practice as a kaleidoscope of surface experiences. Zipping between soaring, transcendent consumption-fuelled highs and aching, despairing lows is the way of postmodern life. But even amid this schizophrenic haze, there is a discipline to the absurdity, a logic of social control that was not there previously. Leisure is no longer a site of freedom (if it ever was); all leisure is consumption. It is the market that is always looking to pitch us into a fascinating but ultimately domesticated leisure experience, which is prepackaged for our individual consumption. What this suggests is that in postmodernity leisure is marked by the individualization of consumer patterns and life itself is consumed by patterns of individualization.

If modernity was a world of men and women beset by fear that they would never arrive, but would always be passing through, postmodernity is a world in which passing through is an obligation. In his many books on postmodernity Bauman alerts us to the different paths that a postmodern life can take and what he suggests is that men and women are not so much challenged with finding their essential identity as being open to the challenge of making and re-making it; they act, are compelled to act, in a world which is always on the move and where no thing stays the same for very long. Postmodernity is episodic and contingent and life's essential incompleteness doesn't merely invite its denizens to fill its gaps; it compels them to do so. Yet it is also a world of cultural confusion. It is no wonder men and women these days are always on the look out for those leisure experiences which tell them how to live: how to pose, what music to listen to, where to shop, what to eat and drink and where to go for their holidays.

If modernity was the world of the nation state and big government, with the emergence of postmodernity we have witnessed an uncoupling of life from the hard stuff of politics (Bauman, 1999a) – or so it would seem. Postmodernity is a world in which there is little political life, when capitalism without questions takes hold, and inattention is routine, when designer labels and celebrities are the only political emblems and figures to whom men and women are prepared to respond. Others see this shift away from big government in a more positive light, in terms of the identification of emancipatory politics (freedom from oppressive top down state apparatuses) to a 'life politics' negotiated via 'dialogic democracy' in the space of civil society, signalling the opportunity for politics proper.

As I argue in the concluding part of my discussion of postmodernity in *The Sage Dictionary of Leisure Studies* (2009), this last observation has a great deal in common with Bauman's (1992) idea that postmodernity offers intimations of the re-enchantment of everyday life and the idea that, after all, modernity had not 'progressed' as far as it thought it had. It also signals the idea that humankind is still touched by a kind of magic that can change lives, and that love, not rationality, is what will open us to the possibility of as yet unimagined and alternative forms of human happiness. Bauman's message is clear: what we need to do is develop the ability to get away from the dominant re-usable language of consumerism to an alternative discourse that speaks itself for the first time. Instead of greedily consuming, we need to get greedy for the small, true details of life. It is only when we are able to grasp this possibility that we will be able to step clear of our consumer cluttered lives into a new relationship with the world, one that is at once simpler and more profound than our present circumstances allow – the best that leisure can do is help facilitate this kind of magic.

LYOTARD: HYPER-CAPITALISM, CONSUMERISM AND THE PERFORMATIVITY OF LEISURE

However, as we have seen, Lyotard points out that with the emergence of postmodernity we have witnessed the collapse of all grand narratives – including politics. Basically, in keeping with the social, cultural, political and economic changes that are consistent with postmodern change, there has been a conspicuous shift in the way in which knowledge claims come to be legitimated. Bauman (1987) develops his own sociological version of these events in *Legislators and Interpreters*, but what he pays far less attention to in any of his work is Lyotard's argument that the idea of *performativity* is coterminous with this new 'generalized spirit' of knowledge.

Basically, Lyotard's argument is that with the advent of postmodernity, capitalism becomes so pervasive that there is nothing left that is not commodifiable. Inevitability science (like leisure) becomes merely another commodity and in turn *truth* is now determined, not by its ability to tell the *Truth*, but by its exchange value. If modernity stood for the language game of denotation (the difference between true or false), postmodernity stands for an alternative, 'technical' game of efficiency versus inefficiency. As a result performativity becomes the new criterion of the legitimacy of knowledge claims. In postmodernity everybody seems to have a view about what constitutes the *truth* and as a result various 'language games' or 'knowledge claims' are made and these are played out through the 'techniques and technologies' of performativity. For Lyotard, this plurality of competing voices is made possible by the 'performativity criterion' which invokes a scepticism towards any idea or theory which posits universal truth claims.

For Lyotard, then, in postmodernity the status of knowledge is altered and performativity comes to represent a kind of hyper-capitalist efficiency which is able to bring the 'pragmatic functions of knowledge clearly to light and elevate all language games to self-knowledge' (Lyotard, 1984: 114). In Austin's (1962) terminology, truth is now performative rather than constative and the most convincing truth claims are those which the market will determine are the most performatively efficient. In a nutshell, everything in postmodernity, including leisure, has to be judged by its market value and if it doesn't sell, it is not what is wanted, pure and simple. Truth is today in the manner of its performance and the upshot is that if branding was once upon a time solely the language of the market it has now become the language of the world as a whole.

Lyotard describes the advent of postmodernity as an event rather than a movement as such. The function of postmodern leisure (if we can call it that) is not to confirm the pursuit of truth or self-understanding but rather to precipitate the 'now'. One of the upshots of this is that leisure does not require any 'accompanying self-consciousness' (Ferguson, 2009: 181); it is performative rather than expressive. What this tells us is that in postmodernity, it is no longer human consciousness that is the centre of leisure experience, but the body.

Leisure, the body and the cult of the 'into'

Jean Baudrillard's concept of the 'into' is a good example with which to explore this idea of performative leisure. This concept, which I have explored in a number of previous publications (Blackshaw and Crabbe, 2004; Blackshaw and Crawford, 2009), does not permit precise definition. It is tied to Baudrillard's penetrating critique of the 'fatal strategies' of the consumer society in which being 'into' leisure or 'into' sport is not only a manifestation of narcissistic self-love of the body and dedication to the preservation of youth, but it is also something much more than that as well. Implicit (if not explicit) to Baudrillard's thesis of the 'into' is the idea that not only do most of us today feel an inner emptiness in our lives, and that as such we are often given to existential self-doubt, but that the body is a depiction of the dance we do with our own transience, and the accommodations we make with ourselves in order to just get through the day. In this sense, we believe that being 'into' the body will operate almost to protect us against predictable fatefulness death. The upshot of this is that the way that we have become phobically concerned with the body prefigures the way in which it will be made up in the 'funeral parlour on our death': 'where it will be given a smile that is really "into" death'.

The point is not to be, nor even to have, a fit body, but to be 'into' your own body, 'into' your sexuality, 'into' your desire. With the hedonism of the 'into', the body is a 'scenario'; the curious 'hygienist threnody' (lamentation for the dead) devoted to it runs through the innumerable fitness centres, and gyms, bearing witness to a mass individualist asexual obsession. As Baudrillard suggests, 'this is how it is with body-building: you get into your body as you would into a suit of nerve and muscle. The body is not muscular, but muscled. It is the same with the brain and with social relations of exchanges: body building, brainstorming, word-processing' (quoted in Horrocks, 1999: 54). A similar scenario surrounds joggers and jogging:

> you can stop a horse that is bolting. You do not stop a jogger who is jogging. Foaming at the mouth, his mind riveted on the inner count down to the moment when he will achieve a higher plain of consciousness, he is not to be stopped ... Jogging is a form of self-torture ... Like dieting, bodybuilding and so many other sports, jogging is a new form of voluntary servitude (it is also a new form of adultery).
>
> (Baudrillard, 1989: 37–8)

Consequently our expenditure of energy is no longer related to work but to leisure, to 'gymtime', where the virtually disabled ... can work off 'stress' in body-building, step-classes or other novel exercise regimes. In the gym, as we work-out, the video screens dominate. And everyone is aware of this. According to Baudrillard, no performance can be without its control screen and what he describes as the New International Hygienic Order wants to be seen and is 'everywhere jogging or walking, phobically concerned with bodies, self-maximization and self-inflicted servitude ... There are no more heights – just dangerous sports' (Horrocks, 1999: 55–6).

Baudrillard is also concerned here with a contemporary obsession with risk which is symptomatic of the contemporary world. First, material risk is *individualized* as the responsibility of the nation state to its populace diminishes while at the same time the global network of capital and commodities continues to grow independently of international borders. Second, 'new' risks abound. The contemporary world is the age of global warming, terrorism, HIV and AIDS, CJD, BSE, SARS, H1N1, to name but a few 'new' risks. These risks take on an added dimension when we take into account the central importance of body-cultivation discussed above, which means that we now not only pay more attention to the body, but also to anything that it is consumed by, or that comes into contact, with it. This is what Bauman (1994:154) calls the postmodern 'horror of disease and toxic substances that [may vandalize the individual] by entering the body or touching the skin'. These observations notwithstanding, Baudrillard takes Bauman's observation one step further, by suggesting that predestined to exact both physical and symbolic violence on the self, the individual invents extreme *risks* rather than face their destiny and in the process fritters him or herself away in an 'exhaustion of possibilities'. A good example of this is edgework.

Edgework and leisure

This concept, as an expression of the ways in which people use leisure activities to deal with the 'edge' – the boundaries between order and disorder, life and death, consciousness and unconsciousness, subject and object – in the pursuit of voluntary risk taking and adventure, owes a great deal to Turner's (1973) work on liminality which we discussed in Chapter 2. Edgework is not a postmodern idea *per se* and it might be best understood as another kind of extreme leisure. But what makes it interesting to debates about postmodern leisure is its status as a legitimating reference point for those involved. That is, those who engage in edgework do so, not because it is a revered leisure pursuit, but because it is effective, it works. In other words, like the famous wood sealant, it does what it says on the can. As I argue in *The Sage Dictionary of Leisure Studies* (2009), expounded in the work of Stephen Lyng (1990; 2005), the general principle of edgework signals the idea of getting as near as possible to the 'edge' without going over it. A good example of this is 'eyeballing', a term used by skydivers to determine the point when their parachute should be opened before 'ground rush' begins.

Written as a response to the limitations of psychologically reductionist accounts of risk taking behaviour which operate with the tacit assumption that feeling alive is only possible in the presence of death, Lyng offers a sociological understanding of edgework that takes into account the ways in which individuals engage in extreme sports but also abnormal leisure activities, such as risky sex, which typically involve observable threats to their physical or mental well-being or 'sense of ordered existence'.

Lyng (2005) argues that the paradox of edgework is that, for some individuals, it signals a way of freeing themselves from the social conditions that stifle the human spirit through social regulation and control, while for others it valorizes the risk taking skills and activities which are demanded by the institutional structures of the risk society – the paradox being that some people seem to be pushed towards edgework practices while others are pulled. Lyng argues that we should not see these two ways of thinking in this 'edgework paradox' as mutually exclusive or incongruous, but as a theoretical amalgam which helps us to better understand the ways in which individuals deal with the ambivalent relationship between freedom and security in the pursuit of play, 'particularly those forms of play that involve both risk and skill', in the contemporary world. To this extent Lyng argues that edgework not only emphasizes an element of personal control in the pursuit of action, but is also a rational and restorative practice, which if it enables individuals to respond to the sense of helplessness they face in the light of the risk society, appears to them as an 'innate response arising from sources deep within the individual, untouched by socializing influences. Thus edgeworkers experience this action as belonging to a residual, spontaneous self, the "true self", as it were' (1990: 879). What this suggests is that edgeworking in leisure is wrapped up with the postmodern search for authenticity in a world that is for many people experienced as inauthentic.

The idea that edgework has the potential to lead individuals to encounter some sort of transcendence, wherein they penetrate the very meaning of life itself to experience an unfettered or authentic sense of self, is challenged by the ambivalence of 'postmodernism', however, which suggests that not only are limit experiences transient and lacking depth – people think they are living on the edge, but in reality they are firmly middle of the road – but also that any idea that the self can have a 'solid' ontological status is itself illusory.

THE POSTMODERNITY OF THE LEISURE LIFE-WORLD OF 'THE LADS'

This theme of the dialogical self is one that I explore in my book *Leisure Life* (2003). The thesis is developed through a hermeneutic sociological approach to make knowable the leisure life-world of a group of working-class 'lads' with whom I had grown up. This meant that the study was about their leisure life-world, my leisure life-world, but also our leisure life-world. Consequently as a researcher I occupied a strange dual position in 'the lads'' universe – Tony Blackshaw as an insider and Tony Blackshaw the sociologist as an outsider on the inside. I used this special position to not only make sense of how 'the lads' live their leisure lives, but to allow the reader to know how they and we *feel* that collective experience, individually together. In particular, the book explores how in their leisure men show a deep interest in what constitutes an authentic self. In other words, how collectively people explore, through their leisure, the deepest questions of selfhood, self-knowledge and personal authenticity.

The crux of my thesis is that 'the lads' may not live in Rojek's Modernity 1 and 2 anymore – likely never have – but their collective consciousness still dwells there and the universe that is their leisure life-world is framed by that ambivalent discourse. The discourse of the leisure life-world follows Kierkegaard's dictum that we live forwards but understand it backwards. Even though the wider world which they *individually* inhabit has become postmodern, in their leisure lives 'the lads' are still animated by their belief in the security of the past which is perceived as the cornerstone of their shared masculine working-class existence. In their leisure 'the lads' find themselves transported to a world in which time stands still and space is dissolved. There is a warmth, a particular feeling of home about this leisure life-world which offers 'the lads' a protective cocoon where they are 'naturally' safeguarded from the uncertainties of postmodern change. They close its shutters to guard against their mutual home-made models of themselves losing credibility and the intricate cogs of their masculine realism from being damaged or lost. The leisure life-world enables them to keep these ready-made narratives alive in their collective memory, their own private gallery, which is the legacy of their youth.

My central argument is that it is this shared passion for a missing world, sometimes proudly resurrected and celebrated, sometimes merely borne out of the private burden of individuality, which gives this shared leisure life-world its depth. The book charts 'the lads'' intermittent forays into Leeds city centre on Friday and Saturday nights which constitute a memorable vindication of this missing world. Nights out with 'the lads' tend to spin themselves out into a familiar web which feels like one of those re-unions which famous rock bands have when the group get back together after playing with other people. When 'the lads' are on stage together once again it feels great and everything just clicks into place. They drink their beer faster than is good for them and conversation moves from subject to subject. They finish each others' sentences, and communicate, more remarkably, without speaking at all. With a real affinity, and in the spirit of the communion that exists between them, they use gestures known only to them. They drink and they drink. As the evening moves on they feel themselves become fully one, the leisure life-world's machinations in fine fettle.

However, on these nights out 'the lads' do not so much re-live their youth as recreate through their leisure its unheroic aftermath. In truth the leisure life-world has, to use the rock band analogy once again, been turned into a sort of heritage museum for ageing lads, which in recent years has become more a duty than a pleasure and whose nagging subliminal power reverberates only on the edges of individual lives lived in the main elsewhere. Indeed, although it is the ultimate experience of what I call a 'solidly modern' leisure life they desire, but cannot really capture, it does not deter them from endeavouring to regain the power and certainties of its past, and seeking a realm of mutual happiness that was once upon a time theirs.

Outside the leisure life-world, resignation and disillusionment are the nearest things 'the lads' have to freedom. In the fluidity of a world marked by postmodern change they have to watch powerless as the Other invades uninvited into their existential and material realms: women controlling their bedrooms and telling them what to do, women and black people taking their jobs, buying their houses, taking over their shops and their schools. But in the leisure life-world 'the lads' are in control. Here the features of the Other begin to elongate and liquefy, swell and then re-solidify, like Sartre's *le visqueux,* they are transformed into 'the lads'' own DIY custom-made creations. Take for example, women, who can never exist as cheerful subjects of their own lives in the leisure life-world, but are instead constituted by 'the lads' as 'birds', 'slags' and 'fanny' living 'solidly' modern lives, excluded from the discourse which creates their identities ready-made. That these characterizations are not 'real' is neither here nor there, 'the lads' simply have to be convinced that they are. What is important for 'the lads' is the *meaning for them* of these characterizations to their version of truth, which is something that enables them to form what they recognize *is* the world when they are at leisure together. In other words, the Other is wiped out from a modern story in which it has no place, excluded from the leisure world that has created it. These characterizations of the Other become symbols of subjugation, power and knowledge, the luscious fruit of a 'solid' leisure life lived in a 'solid' version of truth. This is the 'universal' truth of the rationality which divides 'the lads' and Others into two categories: us and them, same and Other.

In the leisure life-world 'the lads' have the best of both worlds: they have their myth and are able to relativize it as a *contingent* leisure experience, which has its own monologic. Indeed, the modus operandi of this leisure life-world always presumes this form of closure: the conformation of hegemonic masculinity and the restoration of disrupted stability, which provide intimations of the past world of communal bliss in a protected time space in which 'the lads' attempt to impose the fixity of a masculinist, working-class myth on to the ostensible fluidity of postmodern life.

As we get to know 'the lads', and the leisure life-world shuttles backwards and forwards in time, it becomes evident that the idyll is not what it seems. 'The lads'' apparently granite authenticity isn't at all what it seems. In common with other postmodern men and women they find it difficult to remain authentic for long because they simply have too many other choices in their lives. 'The lads' know that the weekend experience of this life-world is just a leisure break; they understand this and are resigned to their fate. In the event it is only because of its own impossibility that the leisure life-world is possible at all. 'The lads' may be figures carved in the past, but their identities are maintained in the present and, in common with other postmodern men and women, they are *individuals* first and all the rest after. In the words of Bauman, it is this observation that represents the 'irreparable and irredeemable ambivalence' of the leisure life-world of 'the lads'.

Deconstructing the leisure life-world of 'the lads'

What I offer the reader in this book is essentially a story about a leisure life-world and its intuitions, a sense of something that is more than meets the eye, a glimpse of how hermeneutics powered by the postmodern imagination can provide sociology with an alternative way of understanding how people use their leisure. It is a book that wishes to do one thing and another: it is both sociological hermeneutics (i.e. systematic and analytical) and hermeneutic sociology (i.e. simply the sparkling statement of a valuable point of view): it says one thing and another. Importantly, it says something about men and their leisure from a non-neutral place, and in the context of its contingent reality.

In this way the compositional practices of hermeneutics offer creative ways of telling factual stories. This suggests a shift in the writing of empirical research, which means that if hermeneutics is as compelled as orthodox sociology ever was in its ambition to capture everyday life, it also has an ambition to create atmosphere, whether it is a single consciousness or the atmosphere of a shared consciousness – even the consciousnesses of postmodern leisure lives that are contingent, shape-shifting rather than enduring. In my book I argue that it is only by such staging that researchers can reach a more profound level of truth that cannot otherwise be found. This is because hermeneutics relishes the task of transporting its readers by telling them how people who share a particular fate think, speculate, desire, understand, live their leisure lives, but in a way which makes every gesture, every attitude, every word spoken by its respondents, part of its imaginative and deliberate study.

By alternating perspectives in the book, seeing events unfold through 'the lads'' eyes and then from the view of the research, I try to do more than simply analyse this leisure life-world; I also attempt to coax the reader into walking in the shoes of 'the lads' to 'lad-like' experience their worldview. The leisure life-world is more real than the flesh and blood characters that are 'the lads'; its discourse more alive, more interesting and more nuanced than the characters speaking it. This is nothing less than about reinventing the empirical researcher's writing craft by making 'fact' read like 'fiction', using language charged and poetic, which takes its readers on a cultural ride in order to find truth – physically transporting them. In other words, the postmodern imagination shakes and wakes leisure studies and in the process, doesn't so much attempt to define and describe the world it comes across in the field as an objective reality, but instead attempts to give it its own living, breathing presence, by summoning it alive through the medium of language. Here, 'reality' is availed of its inability to speak for itself. In this way hermeneutics permits and requires greater descriptive detail than is the case in more conventional empirical leisure studies accounts.

CRITICISMS OF POSTMODERN UNDERSTANDINGS OF LEISURE

There are critics who will no doubt argue that the borrowed prestige of fiction can limit as well as liberate leisure studies. That is, to liken leisure studies to literature may suggest that it verges on fiction. But such a reaction fails to recognize that even the most positivistic of accounts are prey to cosmetic enhancement. What the postmodern imagination tells us is that the real world is contingent, chaotic and crowded with inessentials while leisure studies requires order, themes and structure, so researchers can transform the accumulation of their experiences into an object of analysis. 'One of the upshots of this', the critic might ask, 'is that there must be a temptation to sharpen an observation here or make better a quote there.' What such criticism ignores is that this kind of thing can be tempting to *any* researcher. Readers do not have to be reminded that they are reading 'fact': but hermeneutics shows them how close facts relate to fiction.

The critic might retort: 'At what point does fact pass into the fiction?' In *Leisure Life* I sidestep this question by stressing that this hermeneutical way of writing empirical research should not be understood in any way as deceitful on my part, but more precisely as leisure studies looking at itself in the mirror and recognizing that it can still do everything it used to be able to do *and* much more. The trick of hermeneutics is that it is able to tell the 'truth' about the social world while not being exactly deceitful, but furnishing that 'truth' with its own sense of the world. In this way, rather trying to make the reader believe in the 'facts' of the reality it deals with in its pages, the postmodern imagination simply conjures the 'real' instead. This changed economy of narration simply leads researchers such as myself to write in self-consciously literary ways, which tend to draw on metaphor, which we use *not* to replace the real, but to clarify, reinforce and enhance our understanding of it. In order to get to grips with the leisure life-world of 'the lads' all you have to do is accept a world which is figurative. In other words, in the place of methodological reliability and validity there is only the literariness of hermeneutics, which holds its own uncomplicated magic – the kind that can't be deconstructed.

These observations notwithstanding, one particular, and often voiced, criticism, is that 'postmodernism' goes too far and that 'postmodernists' have a tendency to reduce everything to self-conscious cleverness and irony. To paraphrase Zbigniew Herbert, they forget that irony is just like salt: you crunch it between your teeth and enjoy a short-lived delight; when the delight has gone, though, the brute facts of reality are still there (cited in Coetzee, 2009b: 25). In other words, these critics complain that postmodernists discuss the world only in aesthetic terms and don't engage with its deeper, material content and that

> by focusing on pleasures, fantasies and pastiche, postmodernism neglects many people's lives which remain influenced by the experiences of poverty, gender and racism. This is political and social reality and if we are to study and understand leisure in times of change we must explore postmodern leisure but without losing sight of persistent social inequalities.
>
> (Scraton and Bramham, 1995: 34)

Yet rather than advancing a convincing criticism of 'postmodernism', Scraton and Bramham simply set 'it' up as a straw target. The underlying problem with their critique is that it mistakes the postmodern imagination for cultural relativism or negative 'postmodernism'. This is wide of the mark. As I have demonstrated in this chapter those studies inspired by the postmodern imagination give due attention to those important aspects of leisure – pleasure, fantasy, happiness, desire, and all the rest besides – which are too often conspicuous by their absence in leisure studies. The way that they do this is not at the expense of ignoring social inequality. On the contrary, the postmodern imagination merely provides them with alternative ways of making meaning that are not 'classed', 'gendered' or 'raced', and which pay people the compliment of taking them seriously as individuals and communities with moral intelligence.

CONCLUSION

We are now in a position to sum up the discussion developed in this chapter. The main themes associated with the postmodern leisure are:

- the idea that it is convergence of the contingent and the inevitable that alerts us to the ambivalence of human being-in-the-world is essential to understanding the postmodern imagination;
- the postmodern imagination teaches us that the world (and leisure) is never what it seems at first sight;
- things were never simple before postmodernity, but they *appeared* to be: the class struggle; men versus women; black versus white; work versus leisure; unfreedom versus freedom;
- the roots of postmodern rootlessness can be found in modernity, which tells us a great deal about the ambivalence that is inherent to (post)modern life;
- the precarization tendencies emanating from differentiation and de-differentiation challenge leisure scholars to place people's *experience* of leisure at the centre of their analyses;
- leisure is often experienced as 'decentred' and needs to be analysed accordingly;
- leisure might be finite in time and space but it is unending in its feeling;
- leisure is increasingly experienced in pointillist time;
- in postmodernity individualization is reflexive which some theorists argue means that the body, rather than consciousness, is the subjective centre of leisure experience;
- the legitimating reference point for 'truth' is no longer the legislating standards set by science, but performativity, i.e. if something works it is true;

- play can be seen in a new light: 'play' means to 'perform' in postmodernity, but it nonetheless also invites the tendency to playfulness;
- hermeneutics rather than grand theory is the basis of the postmodern imagination and its means of rendering meaning.

Two conclusions may be reached. First, straw target criticisms of 'postmodernism' do not stand up to critical scrutiny. Second, the postmodern imagination offers an alternative perspective to grand theory which gives due weight to *both* the aesthetic and the material factors which influence the ways that men and women experience leisure, while recognizing that they imagine and define the world the way that *they* live it, not how leisure studies theorists suppose they do.

Part III

TOWARDS A THEORY OF LIQUID LEISURE

INTRODUCTION

In the previous chapter one of my principal concerns was to ensure that the reader did not misunderstand the true character of the postmodern imagination. Far from being an eccentricity of cultural relativism, or just another 'ism', it should be best understood as the continuation of *skholē* by an alternative means. In this final part of the book, I want to put some conceptual flesh on my argument that in the postmodern imagination there are certain intrinsic features which permit us to see leisure in a new light, and not only that, but also that it provides us with a moral framework to live by, which is governed by very different rules from those that pertain to a modern society built on social class lines.

The difficulty with using the postmodern imagination as the basis of this re-theorization, however, is that, as we saw in the last chapter, it is largely derided in leisure studies, and not only that, but it also suggests that leisure must be understood through the modernity/postmodernity dualism. In order to overcome these two problems, I shall articulate my ideas through Bauman's (2000a) metaphor of liquidity. What this will allow me to do is give appropriate attention to the contingencies – the vagaries of chance encounters and associations – that often produce radical and unintended changes in people's lives. Like Bauman I am emphatic that at the start of the twenty-first century there has been a profound existential shift in the art of life, which can no longer be explained purely in orthodox sociological terms, as something you can merely apply tried and tested concepts to; on the contrary, liquid modern lives have been transformed: they are not only difficult to predict in advance, but also come with infinite possibilities. As I pointed out at the end of Chapter 4, acknowledging that this is the way it will always be from now on is what leisure studies have to face up to.

It is my contention that in the liquid modern world we live in, which is founded first and foremost on freedom, leisure moves steadily into its position as the principal driving force underpinning the human goal of satisfying our hunger for meaning and our thirst for giving our lives a purpose. This is the job leisure was always cut out for, since it is that distinct realm of human activity which perhaps more than any other provides us with the thrill of the search for something and the exhilaration of its discovery. But as we have seen in the preceding chapters of this book it had to wait a long time, until the last few decades of the twentieth century to be precise, to secure this function, which was hitherto occupied by work. Even well into the twentieth century the demands of both paid and domestic labour were such that for many men and women there was simply too little freedom for leisure.

As I also argued in Chapter 4, with the emergence of liquid modernity there has also been a shift from a structured and structuring society in which our identities were largely predetermined by our social class, gender and 'race' to one in which *individualization* dominates more than anything else, and where our identities always remain a work in progress. Class, gender and ethnicity may still exert some degree of influence on our leisure opportunities, but they certainly do not dictate them. Today we inhabit what is an unstructured sociality (rather than a structured society) in which life is lived *noch nicht* surrounded by possibilities that have not yet been realized. In such a sociality freedom is not just a possibility, but a duty. As Bauman puts it:

> In the last hundred years, the balance has shifted away from Freud's 'too little freedom in exchange for more security'. Now the pendulum moves, in full swing, in the opposite direction. Our common fears, anxieties and nightmares followed suit. Not the Orwellian vision of the jackboot trampling on human face torments us, but that of the trapeze art practised without safety net ... Fear of inadequacy replaced the old horror of conformity. We fear more of being left alone than of being forced.
>
> (Bauman quoted in Blackshaw, 2002: 2)

Bauman's story is one that runs opposite to the story that Freud kept on repeating – a story that was concerned with repression, or in other words, the idea that modern civilization was utterly reliant on individuals constraining their impulses and limiting their need for self-expression and knowing their place in the world. Liquid modernity, Bauman suggests, is a world that is governed by the pursuit of pleasure and happiness; and that these today are held by most people to be a legitimate rights.

Trying to understand this different world, with its different rules, where leisure has now replaced work as the cognitive and moral focus of our lives, is not without its own unique problems and challenges, though. Some of these have their antecedents in the past – most notably in the paddings of privilege and the stereotypes left over from modernity in its 'solid' phase – but most of them are particular to liquid modernity, even if most leisure studies scholars carry on 'business as usual' as if they are not. In so short a space as I have got in the final part of this book, I can only deal with these in so far as they apply to our topic. What I have chosen to do, therefore, is devote the last two chapters to one central objective, which is mapping out my own theory of liquid leisure. I have also chosen to develop my theory against the background of Chris Rojek's (2010) thesis in his new book *The Labour of Leisure*.

THE LABOUR OF LEISURE

Rojek's thesis is basically a critical response to leisure studies and their enduring obsession with the work-leisure couplet. He argues that instead of focusing on whether less work means more leisure, we should instead concentrate on why 'less work means a weaker claim upon scarce resources', and why 'more leisure, if disconnected from questions of distributive justice and social inclusion, tends to end in more standardization, impoverishment of the imagination and the woe of entrapment without an alternative' (p. 181).

Perhaps the most central preoccupation of Rojek's critique, however, is the leisure society thesis. This is a utopian ideal which has undergone considerable debate in leisure studies over the years, but it is often used with little conceptual precision. As an idea it slides between the views of those who merely observe that work is losing its former centrality, and those of its most ardent adherents, who suggest that it is only with the emergence of leisure society proper (rather a society of work based on the work ethic) will humankind be able to realize its fullest and free expression of creativity and sociability. The former view usually pivots on the observation of momentous changes that have occurred since the nineteenth century, suggesting that advances in science and technology have eased the lot of the majority of people, thereby bringing them more time for leisure.

From the early 1970s, this view was associated most notably with the sharp decline in the ideology of social class and the emergence of post-industrial society (Bell, 1973), suggesting that fewer hours in paid work means more time for leisure. As Rojek (p. 20) points out, however, the leisure society thesis might have 'put the study of leisure on the map, but it committed it to studying a landscape that was ideal rather than real, wished for rather than evidence-based'. In other words, it remained an *abstract* utopia, which was contented with expressing its desire of another world without ever really showing us how this might be achieved. The upshot was that leisure society did not take place.

Rojek argues that the central issue for leisure studies today is the same as the one that is central to the idea of a successful modern life: self-government. It is individual responsibility and the choice of careers – work and leisure careers – that are most important, not the ideal of a leisure utopia that cannot help but be missing. In a de-differentiating world in which the things we derive pleasure and happiness from are not fixed, 'work' has become more 'leisure-like' and 'leisure' has become more 'work-like'. It is no surprise that the attributes of 'competence', 'relevance' and 'credibility', which were once upon a time essential to be regarded as a valued worker, are today what enable us to develop and nourish meaningful leisure lives. As he puts it in the concluding paragraph of the book:

> Leisure is not consumption activity, since this is ultimately driven by the capitalist goal of ceaseless accumulation. Nor is it activity designed to distract one from the cares and predicaments of work, since this merely reinforces the domination of the work ethic by condemning leisure to a subsidiary, compensatory function. Leisure is a school for life. The end of schooling is to maintain and enhance competence, relevance and credibility. The successful attainment of this end requires perpetual emotional intelligence and emotional labour. Freedom is for the birds.

(p. 189)

Rojek's thesis can be summarized in two parts: first, leisure is not consumption. Leisure is not compensation for work. Leisure is *skholē* (Rojeck uses the expression *scholē* rather than Bourdieu's version used in this book). Second, 'leisure is a school for life'; self-government is the end. The great strength of Rojek's book is that it applies a seminal observation from Heidegger to leisure, and that is that the most important thing that can be said about it is not about what it might look like in the end, but the ways in which it might challenge us to make decisions about our lives in the present. Rojek's thesis is in this sense in part a manifesto for the potential of leisure to change lives and broaden horizons.

However, the problem with the first part of his thesis is that it is essentially what philosophers would call an appeal to Occam's Razor, which involves 'shaving off' all the unnecessary assumptions we have about leisure through rationalization. In other words we are rationally justified in believing that consumption activity is not true leisure because it is shallow and superficial and quite a recent societal-wide phenomenon, while *skholē* is true leisure because it deep and meaningful and can be traced back to the Greeks. However, this is really fundamentally a value judgement on Rojek's part: there are people like him – critical leisure studies theorists – for whom *skholē* is the true meaning of leisure, and there are many others – mainly ordinary men and women – for whom it is not. The ultimate discriminating factor here is not rational justification at all, but taste. But not everyone's taste counts equally. Bourdieu (1984) argues that the kind of sophisticated self-justification of taste when it is used in this way is a result of the speciously constructed interests of dominant groups, such as intellectuals – what he calls the 'cultural arbitrary'. That intellectuals have the power to classify cultural practices under conditions that put their own tastes to the fore *and* in terms of their own distaste for the tastes of others, means that they ultimately subject less powerful social actors to a kind of symbolic violence, which not only legitimizes the systems of meaning constructed in their own interests, but also maintains extant structures of social inequality. Understood in this light, Rojek's counter-intuitive impression that *skholē* is leisure and consumption activity and compensatory free time activity are not, is at once an elitist and undemocratic conception of leisure – one that we have heard before in this book. It is also in essence an injunction not to seek a more complicated explanation for modern leisure because there is already one available.

The second part of Rojek's thesis is much more compelling. I agree with him that *skholē* is important and that it has a great deal of intrinsic value, and hopefully have demonstrated this throughout this book – and will elaborate what it means in even more detail in the concluding chapter. However, to say that 'leisure is a school for life'; 'self-government is the end' is a tautology. For those intent on enhancing their lives through *skholē*, attributes such as 'competence', 'relevance' and 'credibility' are undoubtedly important, and they do indeed require perpetual emotional intelligence and emotional labour, since these constitute the basis of the kinds of *mutual recognition* that facilitate successful self-government. As Axel Honneth (2002) shows us very clearly, how we realize our identities as modern individuals depends a great deal on the ways we develop self-confidence, self-respect and self-esteem through our 'intersubjective, symmetrical and reciprocal' relationships with others. However, the end of schooling is not the accomplishment of the sorts of attributes that were once upon a time only used to equip us for success in the workplace. S*kholē* must be the means to some other end, which is much more than having the ability to adjust to the de-differentiating trends of a liquid modern sociality.

This begs the question: what is the end of leisure? For Rojek, it can't be freedom, since he thinks freedom is only for the birds. I want to suggest that it is not so much this renunciation of freedom as the end of life that is the problem with Rojek's thesis, so much that it does not pay sufficient attention to fact that the true terrain of leisure is the human imagination, that special way of feeling and seeing, an outlook turned on the world rather than simply reflecting it, which provides us with our own unique window onto the world. This, as I have suggested, comes to the forefront of people's lives in the time of liquid modernity. I will come again to this issue in Chapter 7, but we must first of all deal with Rojek's counterintuitive impression that consumption activity is not leisure. This is the topic of the next chapter.

6

LEISURE AND CONSUMPTION: MCDONALDIZATION OR IKEAIZATION?

In common with many other sociological leisure studies scholars Rojek is pessimistic about capitalism. He can't abide the market, or at least 'the capitalist goal of ceaseless accumulation', which compliments Adorno and Horkheimer's (1944) graven image of us having to accept what the 'culture industry' manufacturers' offer, which is itself another rendition of Weber's (1930) 'disenchanted' world that is characterized by a *deficit of meaning* and an insidious sense of gloom. As is well known, Weber argued that the incessant drive to the accumulation of knowledge and wealth is what underpins modernity. This is because in modern societies rationality and rationalization become all-pervasive, and leisure, like all other distinct realms of human activity, is increasingly rationalized – what Weber called the 'iron-cage of rationalization' – for the major needs of modern society are 'cumulative, quantified and quantifiable' (Heller, 1999).

Weber's ideas were developed over 100 years ago, but as we have seen throughout this book the crux of them has been taken up by many scholars. In this chapter, I want to look at George Ritzer's (1998; 2003) contribution to this debate, and in particular his metaphor of McDonaldization. With this he provides the most up to date and perhaps the most compelling application of Weber's ideas to the more recent societal changes and technological advances associated with liquid modernity. Importantly what he also provides us with is a theory with which to 'test' Rojek's assumption that consumption activity is not true leisure. In this chapter, I argue that the understanding of consumption adopted by Rojek acquiesces, like Ritzer's thesis, to the conceptual power of Weber's original putative insights and in so doing massively oversimplifies both the meaning and the purpose of consumption in the lives of modern men and women. In developing this critique the McDonaldization thesis is juxtaposed with my own alternative IKEAization thesis.

THE MCDONALDIZATION OF LEISURE

The first thing to point out is that McDonaldization is not a description of reality, but an *ideal type* or analytical tool that we might use to try to understand those aspects of the world which remain for most of us agonizingly confused, contradictory and incoherent (Bauman, 2007). It can be defined as the process by which the principles of the global fast-food restaurant McDonald's are progressively dominating more aspects of society – including leisure – as well as having a significant bearing on the way that globalization works. The key distinction between McDonaldization and Weber's original thesis is that Ritzer argues that the principal form of rationalization is assumed by the flexible, global corporation, best exemplified in the fast-food giant, rather than the more rigid, large bureaucracy of the state. However, Ritzer draws on the key aspects of Weber's work to demonstrate how rationality and rationalization through McDonaldization pervade everyday life to the extent that they are little by little producing, out of the world we have to live in, a 'disenchanting' world that we might not want to live in, but appear not to be able to do much about. Ritzer's thesis is well known and here I shall merely summarize its key principles.

According to Ritzer (2003: 138) the essence of the McDonaldization process is distinguished by five essential dimensions. The first of these is *efficiency*, 'or the effort to discover the best possible means to whatever end is desired'. A McDonaldizing society is a speeded up, time conscious and consumption based society and consumers expect to be served promptly and efficiently. In order to make this possible McDonald's and its customers strike a deal. The fast food corporation puts into place an inventory of norms, rules, regulations and structures to ensure that its employees perform as efficiently as possible and its customers react by dining in a similar manner. The 'drive-thru' window is the example Ritzer usually uses to illustrate this dimension.

The second dimension concerns *calculability*. This emphasizes quantity – perhaps best personified in the 'Big Mac' burger – which is often accompanied with the loss of quality. Time is of the essence here. Just as the efficiency of McDonald's staff is measured by the speed in which they can produce food and serve it to customers, so McDonald's restaurants are designed to coerce customers not to stay around for too long after they have finished eating. As we have seen, the expectation is that ideally they will buy 'drive-thru' and not come into the restaurant at all.

The third dimension is *predictability*. Not only is it expected that McDonald's products and services will be the same the world over – a Big Mac is always a Big Mac – but so also will be the McDonaldization experience. In another book, Ritzer (2004) likens the predictability found in McDonald's restaurants to what Marc Augé (1995) calls *non-places*, which in marked contrast to places (those topographical sites loaded with substance) are merely repositories of liquid flows, or what he call 'nullities', globally conceived and controlled and lacking the distinctive substance – conversation, flexibility, localism, humanity – that make experiences, products and services real. In other words, McDonaldization is too superficial to be authentic.

The fourth dimension of McDonaldization is *control*. In explaining this Ritzer turns to technology and the example of French-fry machines: just as McDonald's employees are controlled by the bell that rings to tell them when the chips are cooked to just the right colour and texture, so customers are controlled by their inability to choose well-cooked chips.

The final aspect of McDonaldization is the *irrationality of rationality*, which also affects both employees and customers. Basically, in the process of rationally organizing its business McDonald's ends up removing all the things that make work rewarding and eating (read: leisure) a pleasurable experience. The upshot of this is dehumanization: 'Employees are forced to work in dehumanizing jobs and customers are forced to eat in dehumanizing settings and circumstances. The fast-food restaurant is a source of degradation for employees and customers alike' (Ritzer, 2003: 141).

Ritzer himself often refers to the package holiday as the exemplary application of McDonaldization to leisure (Harris, 2005), but as Rojek (2005: 208) demonstrates, the scope of this metaphor is far reaching in its application and 'McLeisure' encompasses a broad range of leisure activities including:

- *Shopping centres/malls*: provide an 'assembly line' experience of shopping based in predictability, uniformity and standardization.

- *Convenience foods:* offer a streamlined, predictable, efficient experience of food consumption. Micro-wave foods 'mechanize' and 'quantify' the process of food preparation by timing the process of cooking.
- *Theme parks*: control and monitor the consumption of leisure space and time. Theme parks employ systems of queuing that are akin to a 'conveyor belt' system. Seeing sights is based in the principle of efficiency which discourages lingering or wandering off on your own.
- *Television:* schedules and increasingly programme content is driven by the ratings war. This involves the predominance of calculability and quantitative over qualitative criteria.
- *Sports*: measuring and monitoring sports performance is now a standard feature of sports organization. Sports stadiums increasingly utilize standards of predictability as a feature of design. For example, domes and artificial turf aim to minimize disruption caused by the weather. Processes of queuing and seating adopt 'assembly line' standards of efficiency and predictability.

Ritzer's metaphor is significant for a number of reasons. Two are especially worth mentioning for our purposes. First, McDonaldization is not just another cunning business model. As Bauman (2000b: 234) points out, 'there must have been a fertile soil for the seed, once sown, to grow so quickly resonant (indeed, a degree of mutual adequacy) between the changes in the existential conditions of postmodern individuals and the escape-from-uncertainty-through-designed-standards which McDonaldization is all about'. Second, McDonaldization shows us that the difference between consuming and leisure is 'getting more blurred by the day and for many practical purposes has been already obliterated'.

THE LIMITATIONS OF THE MCDONALDIZATION THESIS

Ritzer's metaphor has been much debated and there are a number of *general* criticisms of it that can regularly be found in the literature. This is not the place to provide an exhaustive discussion of these criticisms as the inventory is much too long, encompassing the full range of social, economic, cultural, political and ethical implications and connotations of Ritzer's work (see, for example, Alfino *et al.*, 1998). Here we will only discuss some *general* criticisms of McDonaldization in so far that they highlight its main deficiencies *specifically* for understanding leisure.

The idea of McDonaldization is – just like Weber's original thesis – in large measure depressing. It is a highly speculative metaphor, and its incorporation of (post)modernity into the ideal type just described is dubious to say the least. This has led a number of commentators to criticize Ritzer for failing to provide solid empirical evidence for his theorizing. That is, like many other people, Ritzer has obviously spent some time in McDonald's, observing how its business concept works in action in order to build his evidence, but he doesn't appear to have researched in any great depth the relationships between 'the changes in the existential conditions of postmodern individuals and the escape-from-uncertainty-through-designed-standards which McDonaldization is all about', identified by Bauman above.

McDonaldization emphasizes the point that not only is our leisure circumscribed by rational systems that we have little control over, but also that the cultural standardization and normalization of experience these present us with is inevitable (Rojek, 2005). If, in Foucault's language, McDonaldization expresses a particular combination of power and knowledge, then this does not vary between different national configurations; this is because it is able to cater efficiently for needs that as Weber explained are 'cumulative, quantified and quantifiable'. The upshot of rationalization through McDonaldization is the *homogenization* of leisure. Those who want to be themselves in their leisure have to overcome the feeling of 'disenchantment', throw off 'the iron cage' mentality pressing down on them and find their own authentic voices – but this is unlikely since the progressive accumulation of McDonaldization is an infinite process.

However, the notion that employees and customers simply acquiesce to the roles ascribed to them by McDonaldization is open to theoretical reductionism; that is, Ritzer reduces practical knowledge to theoretical knowledge and ignores the fact that, whatever its dark side, leisure, like culture, is praxis (Bauman, 1999b). On the one hand, Ritzer seems to assume that we do not have the necessary skills to outwit McDonaldization and we passively accept its authoritarian powers and, on the other, that we do not want products and services with a human face. He also ignores the possibility that people might seek alternatives to the irrational, anti-social and dehumanizing effects of McDonald's. A good example of this is FC United of Manchester, a community-based football club set up by a collective group of fans who withdrew their support from Manchester United as a result of a corporate takeover (Brown *et al.*, 2008).

This leads us on to the two foremost criticisms of Ritzer. First, just like Weber, he assumes that modernity is a 'disenchanted' world, which is characterized by a *deficit of meaning*. However, by turning away from everyday life to theory, both Weber and Ritzer choose not to focus on the freedoms and the opportunities that modernity offers us by focusing instead on its ostensible deficits. Contrary to what Weber and Ritzer suggest, liquid modernity, especially, is characterized by a *surplus of meaning*. Indeed, in the last 30 or so years we have witnessed an exponential growth in leisure, and importantly, not just the kind that is provided for our consumption through rational expert systems. Most of these new leisure opportunities might not be entirely divorced from commercialization (as we saw in Chapter 5, Lyotard suggests it is by now impossible for them not to be), but many of them are marked with a significant degree of meaning – vocation, innovation and devotional practice – rather than merely reflecting cynical attempts by rational systems to 're-enchant' a modern world that has lost its aura by 'adding leisure values' (Harris, 2005). Examples that fit this trend include brewing real ale, growing fruit and vegetables in allotments, eco tourism, and much else besides. What is also significant about these new leisure trends is the way in which people work to create through their leisure interests new synergies that carry both the weight and the meaning of culture. To take just one example, the traditional Punjabi musical and dance form of Bhangra has been taken up by many young Asian musicians in Britain, who have fused it with a vast range of other musical forms (often hybrids themselves) such as disco, techno, house, raga, jungle and hip hop, to create new sounds and dance forms that are now being re-exported back to Asia.

Second, McDonaldization is simply not sophisticated enough to be the principal driving force of the consumer society. It appears to be because Ritzer tells us everything that matters about consumerism for McDonaldization. But he never gets far with saying what matters about consumerism for ordinary men and women. Contrary to what Bauman suggests (2000b: 234) it is the global home furnishing corporation, IKEA, not McDonaldization, that 'is most seminal of the many present-day trends since it augurs, or brings in its wake, a thorough revolution in business practice as well as in the most essential aspects of daily-life culture', because this is the metaphor that truly reflects our actual experiences of consumerism.

THE IKEAIZATION OF LEISURE

During the last 30 years IKEA has had a massive influence on the development of the business of the home furnishing market, turning furniture into a fashion item, while making it affordable and disposable (Simmons, 2005). As Simmons points out, the designation 'IKEA' stands for Ingvar Kamprad Elmtaryd Agunnaryd. Ingvar Kamprad is the name of the man who founded the company in the 1940s, who grew up on a farm called Elmataryd, in a village in Sweden called Agunnaryd. IKEA's corporate identity is a simple one, ostensibly based on Kampard's philosophy of wanting to 'create a better everyday life for the majority of people', through a commitment to good design at a price that suits its customers, while promoting a sound social and environmental image. It simply recognizes the fact that consumers operate with the entitlement to enjoy the products of someone else's labour.

The IKEA brand is a good example of what Rojek (2010) refers to as *neat capitalism*. Through this term Rojek identifies the knowing, deliberate attempts by entrepreneurs such as Ingvar Kamprad to offer clever but cool solutions to pressing social, cultural and economic questions. His use of the term 'neat' here is intended to express the self-aggrandizing manner in which neat capitalism is promulgated and practised, especially the way in which it sells itself as offering 'savvy *stateless solutions'* to the problems of society and the world by drawing on the sentiments of popular imagination.

There is no better example of the success of neat capitalism than IKEA. At the time that Simmons wrote his article in 2005, IKEA had 202 shops in over 32 countries and was printing 145 million catalogues in 48 editions and 25 languages; it had 410 million customers worldwide, 1 million of whom visit its shops everyday; and employed 84,000 staff. Between 1994 and 2005 its income increased from $4.3bn in 1994 to $19.4bn, representing a growth of more than 400 per cent (Bailly *et al.*, 2006); this occurred while the company reduced its prices between 15–20 per cent during the five year period 2000–2005. In achieving this success, contrary to McDonald's, IKEA has not had to sacrifice its integrity, undermine its brand or alienate its customers.

Notwithstanding its axiomatic power as the liquid modern business model *par excellence*, what is hardly commented on, however, is that during its 60-odd year existence, and particularly over the last 15 years or so, IKEA has become the paradigm for understanding changes in all areas of contemporary life. IKEAization has changed the way that people consume. It has helped realign our economic social class system. It has changed the way we interact. It has become part of our social and cultural fabric. Let us consider its key dimensions and how we might apply the metaphor to contemporary leisure.

First, IKEAization emphasizes the essence of the notion *home* (another word for community) in a modern world in which it cannot help but be missing (Bauman, 2001). It answers the ultimate question modernity poses us: how can one find a home when the things that make it so – continuity, warmth, comfort, safety – are always on the cusp of being taken away? The essence of the IKEA brand is the idea that feeling at 'home' is a nourishing antidote to a thoroughly individualized modern life. You cannot beat the wonder and the warmth of a home. This is what makes IKEAization so absorbing: in this metaphor men and women can find a ready-made solution for subtracting themselves from the exhausting experience of being alone in the world. In other words with IKEAization the world becomes homely. Ingvar Kamprad ('home is the most important place in the world') might never have read Gaston Bachelard (1994 *1964*), but like the great French philosopher of the everyday, he recognizes that 'all really inhabited space bears the essence of the notion of home'. You might say that the core business philosophy of IKEA is to give people a home as they have never experienced it before. To this extent, IKEAization, in the mood of Bachelard, stresses the significance of the experience of intimate places for human beings, identifying the interior spaces of the house – bedrooms, living rooms, kitchens, attics, stairs – and the small spaces contained within it – drawers, sideboards, chests and wardrobes, as our 'first world'. As Bachelard puts it:

> Before he is 'cast into the world', as claimed by certain hasty metaphysics, man is laid in the cradle of the house (*sic*). And always, in our daydreams, the house is a large cradle. A concrete metaphysics cannot neglect this fact, this simple fact, all the more, since this fact of value, an important value, to which we return in our daydreaming. Being is already a value. Life begins well, it begins enclosed, protected, all warm in the bosom of the house.
>
> (Bachelard, 1958: 7)

We also see the 'home' in a different way through IKEAization: as a source of self, an enriching collective world. But the products of IKEAization are much more than consumer life-style accessories. In

IKEA stores consumers find what middle-class fans find in the work-ing-class game of association football: the solidity of a 'full rich' working-class life. Indeed, the 'full package' of a way of life which, to quote that most discerning chronicler of the working-class milieu, Richard Hoggart (1966: 33), whose 'core is a sense of the personal, the concrete, the local: it is embodied in the idea of, first, the family, and second, the neighbour-hood'. IKEAization is in this sense an 'imagined community' (Anderson, 1991) which is not only able to offer a form of sharing that transcends all the other partial viewpoints that make up the fragmented sociality that is liquid modernity, but it at the same time allows us all to enter emphatically into it. Indeed, IKEAization is the ultimate utopia because it signifies the idea of a cohesive entity with the common interest of finding a home, a shared culture and apparent sense of purpose, but which is ultimately an uncertain vision of togetherness.

To keep up the class metaphor, what we also get with IKEAization is the lack of restrictions associated with a 'real' working-class life: something that is dispensable. To paraphrase Bauman, men and women 'tend to believe sincerely that what they truly desire is tranquility [of a cosy working-class life] – but they delude themselves: what they are truly after is agitation. What they really crave is to chase the hare, not to catch it. The pleasure is in hunting, not in catching the prey' (2001: 9–10). Indeed, it is the feeling of excitement that accompanies IKEAization that we really relish.

Having said all that, we are all like IKEA customers in that we often do not know what we want. Unable to weigh the warm glow of making a home against the pleasures of immediate gratification we often 'purchase' on impulse. Like all *neat* capitalists, Ingvar Kamprad is well aware of this: even with something ostensibly concrete and enduring like a 'home', there proves to be no permanence in a 'liquid' modern world. This is why IKEAized dreams (just like some of IKEA's more basic furniture) have their own built-in obsolescence, and are never developed with any eye to longevity; it is their short-lived wonder that is their point.

Underneath many of our leisure interests there is this same subcon-scious, which is 'working-class' and not 'middle-class', 'social' and not 'private', and which evinces our need for forming a home or a community around certain symbols, like a sport, for example. A particularly good example of this is Spracklen's study of the sport of rugby league, where to 'be a rugby league supporter in England means to be part of an imagi-nary community of the working class' (Spracklen, 2009: 159). However, for many people, it is also often the case that when community does live in leisure, it lives likewise, devoid of any kind of extended unity save for that *contingently* imposed on immediate events – a victory for the club in an important match. As Bauman's (2001) work suggests, in our leisure we want community individually wrapped for our own individual consumption. Individualized men and women live their lives as if they do not need the support and backing of the world, with its ready made fixtures and fittings, its conventional points of orientation. We are so individualized and independent that we can live our lives anywhere, and wherever our leisure interests lie – supporting Leeds Rhinos – is potentially home: for the time being at least.

Another one of the primary dimensions of IKEAization is its *democracy*. Unlike McDonaldization which seeks uniformity by trying to absorb disparate personalities, IKEAization recognizes that this is an impossible task. Here lies IKEAization's moral aspect: not only is it keen to promote its social and environmental image, but also that it is democratic. There is no *apparent* stratification as such; no fixity of social class, no patriarchal, racial or age hierarchies: it is open to all-comers. As Donald Sassoon puts it: IKEA is the place where 'workers and burghers alike buy the contents of their homes' (2005: 147). Questionable though it may be, it is the assertion that it includes everyone that gives IKEAization its sting. It knows exactly what it stands for, and it is not for the social class society of the past – even if, as we have seen, it offers its customers the warmth and comfort of that past if they wish to purchase it.

Like the actual IKEA product catalogue itself, IKEAization is nothing less than a rewriting of E.P. Thompson's (1968) *The Making of the English Working Class* as 'The Unmaking of the English Social Classes', but with an underlying tone of nostalgia and a twist of irony. If its manifesto is a failed utopia it still carries you powerfully along. Even with the kitsch, IKEAization is still *Paradise Regained* to the *Paradise Lost* of Hoggart's (1966 *1957*) Hunslet. This is because unlike the manifestos of leftist intellectuals such as Thompson, Adorno and Horkheimer, Ritzer and Rojek content to reveal the workings of power, it is not content to leave the world as it is. IKEAization's decentred manifesto recognizes Heidegger's critical observation that modern men and women 'are beings for whom being is a question'. To paraphrase the philosopher Susan Neiman, to this end it operates with the assumption that we want to determine our own world, not merely be determined by it; and not only that, but we also want to stand above the things we consume (quoted in Black, 2009). With this in mind it helps us plan our desires around the way that *we* actually want to live, not the way those intellectuals imagine we live.

This is true of all leisure forms today. IKEAization makes it virtually impossible for them to remain firmly locked into their own circuits of power and privilege – most people have cultivated a cavalier indifference to these. And it is not just social class differences which, to use an expression coined by Jacques Derrida, come under erasure in our leisure. What this means is that leisure forms, such as rock concerts, which were once just the preserve of the young, are now open to everyone. As John Harris (2009) recently put it in his cogent assessment of the annual Glastonbury event in England: "'Glasto" is now everybody's property, holding out the promise of fun for all the family. You can slum it and position yourself at the cutting edge, or take the kids and a picnic.' For 'Glasto', as for IKEAization, it is *coolness* rather than hierarchy that underpins its positioning status.

Third, as we have seen already, contrary to McDonald's, great importance is given to *incalculability* and *unpredictability*. IKEAization emphasizes 'affordable solutions for better living', but not to the detriment of quality ('Who needs a new kitchen with more than good looks?': IKEA kitchens come with a 25 year 'everyday quality guarantee'), diversity ('Everyone's welcome in an IKEA kitchen'), and innovations in style, but not with an expensive price ('Big on style ... Not on price'). Not only does IKEA have its own teams of product designers ('Why do designers work for us? IKEA asks. "Because they are passionately mad."') for coming up with goods it stacks on its warehouse shelves, but it also offers its customers pre-fabricated furniture arrangements which are both 'jaw-dropping' and made to measure in its very own 'have-it-all-approach to affordable design'. IKEAization does what McDonaldization could only dream of: it outstrips the imagination of any consumer. It also fits very nicely the requirements of individual men and women who have little time for waiting at checkout counters and who want to exchange any faulty goods they have purchased with the minimum of fuss.

To briefly apply this dimension to leisure. The transformation of fashion is a good example. Retailers, such as the British billionaire owner of the Arcadia group and Topshop, Sir Philip Green, another *neat* capitalist, have been very successful at offering their own IKEA-type innovations in fashion by making luxury and style 'accessible' to everyone. What Green does better than most other retailers in the fashion business is offer 'individualized' products that mirror the aura of designer clothes on the high street at cheap prices; the trick being to offer luxury and style on the cheap without stripping away what makes it special. He also has an eye for a new market, and not only that, but an acute awareness that people have little time and patience when they shop these days. Anyone who has recently walked into a Topman store will also be aware of their proclivity for playing cool, up-to-the-minute 'indie' music. Topman has recently struck a deal with Rough Trade records to sell 'indie' music in its stores (Bray, 2009). The message is a clear one: come to Topman and find the coolest clothes and coolest new sounds before either one hits the mainstream.

Fourth, IKEA might be a global brand, but unlike McDonald's, there is something inherently *provincial* about its character and this is a cause for celebration. Its lack of US hegemony is a key part of the appeal of IKEAization. Both its customers and its staff ('co-workers') are also seen as an important part of the IKEA 'family' ('Too many cooks? No such thing. We say the more the merrier. When the whole family is together, the kitchen is at its best. Its liveliest. Its cosiest. Its happiest!'). Moreover, it anthropomorphizes its products by giving them Swedish names that charm its customers and to which they can relate: Aneboda (chest of drawers), Ektorp (armchair), Grimen (bed), Mysa Rönn (quilt cover), Pax Ådal (wardrobe), Tuvull (travel rug), and much else besides. In so doing it offers its customers a shopping experience with a homespun, European feel about it, rooted in the experience of the IKEA 'family', and delivered by 'co-workers', who are expected to care. Unlike McDonaldization, IKEAization is warm, intimate and enchanting.

There is a great deal of evidence to demonstrate the seminal success of the IKEA revolution of business practice and its impact on people's daily lives. As Bailly *et al.* (2006) suggest, the strength of bonds between IKEA and its customers are deep and the lengths they will go to shop at IKEA are truly amazing:

> In 2004 a Stockport town councillor in Lancashire, Britain, bragged that having an IKEA store was an honour for the town. At Mougins, in the south of France, local people started a petition which read: 'If you are fed up with making a 200km round trip, lasting two hours, just to shop in your nearest IKEA, then seize this opportunity (maybe the last) to bring a new IKEA to the Alpes-Maritimes department. This is remarkable: people organising a petition, which collected more than 2,000 signatures, standing up for their rights and organising because a furnishing store lacks an outlet within 100km. Of course success on this scale has its downside. When the firm

opened a store in Saudi Arabia in 2004, it offered a $150 cheque to the first 50 shoppers through the door. There was almost a riot, with two deaths, 16 injured and 20 fainting fits.

IKEAization is also unlike McDonaldization in another key way. Fifth, its roots lie not in the hegemony of the cultural practices of USA free-time activity, but in the *Protestant work ethic* (Simmons, 2005). In this sense, it has in common with the American dream which founded on the notion the self-sufficient homestead. Ingvar Kamprad knows that the satisfaction that comes through giving your home an IKEA makeover cannot just be bought: it has to be earned, learned and worked at. As Simmons points out, IKEA's customers recognize the way in which IKEA operates is largely to do with lowering costs and that there is complicity between them and the company to make this business model work. The upshot of this is that IKEA's customers have developed a disciplined and diligent commitment to picking up their own furniture, carrying it home and making it themselves. As Simmons puts it:

> the ideas of 'flat-pack' and 'IKEA' are inseparable. The practicality of the invention meant that transportation costs for furniture could be greatly reduced – and the assembly costs of putting the furniture together could be passed on to the customer. In a sense, this seems an enormous cheek. Yet IKEA customers participate willingly because they understand their role in reducing the price they pay for furniture.

Yet at the same time, and what goes unnoticed by Simmons, is that IKEAization offers the tantalizing prospect of maximum Puritanism for the minimum of sacrifice – another underlying irony.

Crucially, IKEAization also caters for consumers who are looking for something that is a tad more challenging than the straightforwardly 'off the peg': self-assembly can be a bit tricky, and everyone struggles a bit, but with a bit of effort you get there in the end. IKEAization recognizes that the real pleasure of consuming lies in its ambivalence: the enthralment of the search and the exhilaration of discovery. IKEA customers not only get off on acquiring stylish new furniture but also the anticipation and thrill of gaining new knowledge and skills in the process of putting together their acquisitions. As we have already seen, what also makes IKEA attractive to its customers is that its products are as elastic as the tales of its marketing spinners and extendable enough to fulfil whatever dreams they have in mind.

As it was demonstrated in Chapter 3, Weber famously identified the *Protestant work ethic* as the crucial cultural feature in the development of industrial capitalism and we took up the key ideas associated with this dialectical relationship to explain its impact on the productive use of leisure time in the early modern period. The way in which the *Protestant work ethic* becomes discernable with IKEAization is also with the productive use of leisure time. To this extent IKEAization blurs the distinction between serious and casual leisure. In other words, even when leisure is commodified, it does not rule out the fact that it provides men and women with the enthralment and satisfaction that is assumed by Stebbins to accompany only serious leisure activities. This can be seen in Baudrillard's (1989; 1990) idea of the 'into' discussed in the last chapter, which suggests that the point is not to just have a leisure interest, but to be 'into' leisure, which he suggests is a new form of 'voluntary servitude'. This dimension of IKEAization can be seen in the imposition of the strict and punishing regimes in sport, exercise and keep fit, which provides us with a broad range of elaborate ways for refashioning the body. In these ways, we assert our freedom, refuse poor physical limits and transform our bodies (just like our homes) into what we want them to be.

It is in these ways that IKEAization also emphasizes the idea of *coolness*. Most readers of this book will be so familiar with the idea of coolness that they will probably think that it barely needs to be explained. After all it is difficult to imagine anything people do today that is not robed in the idea. Yet for all its popularity, and any ostensible certainty about its origins, coolness is at best an elusive disposition. If ice and fire are binary extremes, coolness is a zombie category somewhere in-between. It is a way of being in the world which is designedly and teasingly (supposed to be) transgressive, but performed in a way that seems to take things neither too seriously nor too lightly. Just as there is no certainty about where coolness is going to be found, or how long it is going to reside there once we've found it, there is no such thing as a hierarchical notion of coolness. It is an attitude governed by a more plural and pragmatic aesthetic: if something works, 'hey, it's cool'. As this suggests, the idea has a renegade quality: not only is it in awe of the idea of non-compliance, but it is also hard to pin down and is governed by an ephemeral currency, susceptible to sudden shifts in the wind.

The cool attitude is the mindset of IKEAization. If the rigid Puritan asceticism was the abiding ethic of a 'solid' modern society dominated by industrial labour, 'liquid' aestheticism is the indispensable centre of coolness. A certain independence from rational evaluation is a critical component of coolness. To talk of something as being intrinsically cool and which is measured by universal standards is to misunderstand its shape-shifting nature – being a cool dresser, a cool dancer, having a cool kitchen or music collection, cool friends, and so on, are difficult to place – because proper effortless coolness has no rational foundations. Rational logic would also suggest that coolness multiplied by coolness should mean something cooler, but in practice, an odd kind of polarizing effect often takes place. Rather than amplifying each other, coolness multiplied by coolness often cancel each other out. There is also the paradox that it can also be coolness to be uncool – for example, revealing to your mates in their twenties that you have a penchant for 1970s 'Glam-Rock' bands.

One of the upshots of the uncertainty surrounding coolness is that it makes our cognitive activities seem somewhat always self-conscious. It is as if we cannot enjoy our own corporeal existence without worrying about whether we look cool or not. This is because in a performative society self-respect must be expressed in a carefully balanced out – neither too hot nor too cold – outward appearance and demeanour. We inhabit a world in which aesthetics rule supreme and where people imagine that they will discover their individual sense of existential empowerment by creating their own chilled out sense of coolness.

The cult of coolness, of cultivating a cool appearance, criss-crosses all aspects of IKEAized leisure: rappers justify their lyrical extremities with it; some football fans found their identities on it; consumers always seem to be on the look out for guides to living that tell them the coolest ways to live and how to pose and what the coolest music to listen to and where to shop for the coolest clothes and what to eat and drink in the coolest restaurants and where to go for the coolest holidays.

What this suggests is that the technologies associated with IKEAization facilitate *freedom* rather than control. As we saw in Chapter 4, Bauman consistently reminds us that consumerism has by now replaced work as the backbone of the reward system and it is only the losers in the liquid modern board game of snakes and ladders – the flawed consumers – who are still controlled through the work ethic. As we have seen IKEAization redraws the boundaries between social class divisions as a relationship between those with different abilities to consume. In an IKEAizing society control is barely noticeable, because there is always something to fit even the smallest budget ('Our biggest idea is the smallest price') and the shallowest commitment (it offers chipboard as well as solid oak furniture). It is this last dimension which perhaps best exemplifies why it is *precarized* IKEAization rather than progressive McDonaldization that is 'the most seminal of the many present-day trends'. To tweak what Bauman said of consumerism generally and what can be applied to IKEAization specifically:

> What makes the freedom offered by [IKEAization] more alluring still is that it comes without the blemish which tainted most other forms [for example, public sector leisure facilities]: the same market which offers freedom offers certainty. It offers the individual the right to a 'thoroughly individual' choice; yet it also supplies social approval for such choice, thereby exorcizing that ghost of insecurity which ... poisons the joy of the sovereign will. In a paradoxical way [IKEAization] fits the bill of the 'fantasy community' where freedom and certainty, independence and togetherness live alongside each other without conflict. People are thus pulled to [IKEAization] by a double bind: they depend on it for the individual freedom; and they depend on it for enjoying their freedom without paying the price of insecurity.
>
> (Bauman, 1988: 61–2)

CONCLUSION

The mantle of the principal driving force of consumer society is assumed by IKEAization. An IKEAized existence is a compelling one. How it works with the ideas of home, community and coolness, and how it makes people feel about themselves, borders on the sublime: it is ordinary and special, within the reach of everybody but somehow, at the same time, out of reach, of some other world. Or is it ridiculous? For Rojek, IKEAleisure cannot be leisure since it is fundamentally consumption. In other words, IKEAization is seductive, but its seduction comes with a price: the loss of freedom, the loss of leisure, the loss of the entitlement to the products of one's own labour. Rojek is wrong. In the language game of leisure, McDonaldization and IKEAization share the family resemblance of being consumerist. However, the key difference between the two is that where in the former consuming is firmly located in the *fixed* 'design-standards which McDonaldization is all about', in IKEAization the relationship is not one way. The reason for consuming is located in a cultural discourse between our own aspirations and the *fluid* and *flexible* design-standards of IKEAization. What this suggests to me is that in the species of leisure known as consuming, IKEALeisure is 'good of its kind'. McLeisure is not.

7

THE AMBIVALENCE OF LEISURE

The second key argument underpinning my theory of liquid leisure is that liquid modernity ushered in a new phase for leisure, which saw it ingeniously empowered by the human imagination. To paraphrase what Agnes Heller (1999: 125) has said about culture more generally, with the onset of liquid modernity, the subsidiary, compensatory function of leisure was transformed to an interpretive function. In other words, leisure has become a hermeneutical exercise. That is, leisure ceased to be defined through the distinction between its good and bad aspects – work against leisure, serious leisure against casual leisure, leisure as freedom against leisure as constraint; instead, it acquired more and more meaning. In liquid modernity, then, it is hermeneutics that deepens the meaning of leisure, rather than good and bad taste or judgement. It is meaning, the appeal to the *unknown known* that places *my* leisure interest at the top of the modern hierarchy of culture. It is placed high by me because it has the potential to serve for infinite interpretability – as well as giving me pleasure and happiness – again and again. In liquid modernity, leisure performs a key function, then: the function of rendering meaning.

The key peculiarity about this change in function is one that Raymond Williams would have called *unaware* alignment turned into *active* commitment, or in other words, the moving of social relationships to human consciousness. Unaware alignment refers to the kind of leisure you are stuck with, i.e. compensatory leisure, while active commitment refers to leisure that we engage in because we *feel* it our duty to do so. This is leisure practice that appeals to the sixth-sense in all of us – that special way of seeing, whose *doxa* we cannot precisely put into words, but which provides us with our own unique window on to the world – which animates us to reach out towards some super-sensible truth, higher than ourselves, that provides us with a purpose for living. This is leisure that also signifies obligation, responsibility, and especially desire. Hermeneutics presupposes that there is *something* about the leisure pertaining to our chosen devotional practice (its *unknown known*) that cannot be disciplined – its *secret* (its *unknown known*). We know that active commitment to our chosen devotional leisure practice is our duty, but its *secret* is beyond interpretation; we do not know, cannot know about its secret; rather we *feel* its warm glow, we *sense* it. Yet knowing all this does not stop us trying to find out its secret. This is the ambivalence of devotional leisure practice.

Interpretation of leisure is a devotional practice. To tweak and add to Heller's (p. 144) narrative once again, the object of devotion is the 'this-ness, the ipseity' of my chosen leisure practice that makes it distinctive from other freely chosen leisure practices. When men and women choose leisure in this way they do so with a sense of feeling, as though it were something holy, as though engaging in it were a religious function. There is more to leisure, this attitude would seem to suggest, than mere leisure activities or recreational pursuits, but to live one's life in a certain way. What I have in mind when I use the term leisure as a devotional practice is something like Weber's idea of a value-sphere, which suggests that not only is leisure governed by a particular set of norms, rules, ethics and obligations that are inherent to it, but also that those who commit themselves to leisure do so as a vocation; the relationship between their life and their leisure is fundamental. In other words, and to paraphrase what Zinzendorf (cited in Weber, 1930: 264, note 24) said about work: in making an existential commitment to leisure men and women not only leisure in order to live, but live for the sake of their leisure, and if there is no more leisure to have they suffer or go to sleep. Two good applied examples from the literature of this kind of devotional leisure practice are Blackshaw and Crabbe's (2004) heterotopia of car cruisers and Spracklen's (2009) 'self-referencing community' built around black metal music, in which action is communicative. But the list is endless since these days any kind of leisure is potentially a devotional practice – even shopping.

There is, however, an essential difference between *skholē* and other interpretations of leisure. *Skholē*, as its nomenclature suggests, is interpreted as sacrosanct, which means that devotion goes not only for what makes it distinctive, but also the authority of the tradition it has behind it. In fact, it turns out that *skholē* is actually hermeneutics since it is its tradition that ties 'us' to the 'other', i.e. its current interpreters to its original interpreters, the Greeks. In the case of all other devotional leisure practices, devotion alone is the basis of authority – the leisure practice in question can only speak for itself.

What this tells us is that the selection of leisure worthy of devotional interpretation is a spiritual practice. Since those who are committed to devotional leisure practices cannot ever know the secret of the source of their spirituality what needs to be determined first and foremost is who is 'us' and to what do 'we' belong. For hard core Leeds United football supporters, for example, one of the ways this synthesis is animated is when the crowd sings 'Marching on together'. There is something in the words that strikes at all Leeds United fans' hearts: they are connected to each other through this. This song is their song. Leeds is their identity: 'We are Leeds, we are Leeds, we are Leeds; We are Leeds, we are Leeds, We are Leeeeds. ...'

There is, however, a critical distinction between devotional leisure practice under the auspices of solid modernity and liquid modernity. Under the auspices of solid modernity spiritual practice was circumscribed by two distinguishing factors: on the one hand, taste, and on the other, the *legislating* power of the keepers of its secret. Judgement of taste was determined by the authority of these legislators. According to Bauman (1987: 4–5), the legislators are those keepers of secrets who make authoritative ideological statements about the world and who have the power to make the '*procedural rules* which assure the attainment of truth, the arrival of moral judgement, and the selection of proper artistic taste. Such procedural rules have a *universal validity*, as to the *products* of their application.' Under the auspices of solid modern conditions, then, it was unlikely that the selection of a devotional leisure practice would be something as tasteless as committing oneself wholly to a football team. Artist endeavours, such as opera, classical music, recreational sports, or even a hobby, such as stamp collecting, maybe, but not supporting a football club.

With the onset of liquid modernity, however, when performativity became the dominant lens through which we view the world, not only was the authority of these keepers of secrets downgraded in importance, but so also was the power of their *legislating* message, their way of communicating truth. These keepers of secrets did not readily give up their legislating authority without putting up a fight, but devotional leisure practice is gradually being replaced by an alternative *interpretive* mind-set, whose authority is more democratic and located in popular culture and the market. While the influence of the legislators has now waned, the DIY peer-to-peer interpretive leisure scene has waxed. One important upshot of this trend is that the hierarchical, depersonalized and detached language of the keepers of secrets has given way to the cool attitude. As we have seen already in the discussion of IKEAization in the last chapter there is no such thing as a hierarchical notion of cool. It is an attitude governed by a more plural and pragmatic aesthetic: if something works, 'hey, it's cool'.

THE INDIVIDUALIZATION OF DEVOTIONAL LEISURE PRACTICE

What the analysis developed so far suggests is that there is a real hunger and thirst for deep, experience-full leisure everywhere these days and all leisure activity, notwithstanding whether it is (re)creation or consumption based, has the potential to be interpreted and worked up into a devotional practice. As we saw in Chapter 2, when we discussed the topic of extreme leisure, devotional leisure practice holds no bounds, stretching from extreme sport to extreme cuisine to extreme pornography. The list is endless. Men and women live their lives with a refusal to be bounded that is almost sentimental in its desire to go on until every possible leisure practice has been explored with the self-same fervour. However, in liquid modernity it is the individual who has the authority to choose devotional leisure practice, not the other way round. Individuals choose their leisure; it is no longer the case that their leisure chooses them.

In marked contrast to devotional leisure practices in solid modernity those developed under liquid modernity are governed by 'the continuation of disembedding coupled with dis-continuation of re-embedding' (Bauman, 2002: 2). The upshot is that devotional leisure is practiced in *pointillist* time which means it is experienced in episodes (Bauman, 2007), and the sense of community we experience with it, when it does live, lives similarly, devoid of any kind of extended unity save for that contingently imposed on immediate events.

With liquid modernity, a postulated unity of interests gives way to more specialized *habitats* and associated life-styles and individuality where men and women become '*operators* who are willing to forego a secure source of fruit for a chance to connect more of the world' (Wellman *et al.*, 1988: 134). Men and women invest their hopes in 'networks' rather than 'communities' of leisure, 'hoping that in a network there will always be some mobile phone numbers available for sending and receiving messages of loyalty' (Bauman, 2006: 70). Consequently, individuals going their own way in a world tend to hook up with other individuals with whom they share common devotional leisure interests to form what Maffesoli (1996) calls neo-tribes, which are reminiscent of Lash's (2002a: 27) 'post-traditional' *Gemeinschaften*, in that they are 'mobile and flexible groupings – sometimes enduring, often easy dissoluble – formed with an intensive affective bonding'. Their affiliation is not really one of friendship, or of a community proper, but one of symbiosis and their only glue is their incumbents' shared devotion.

In this sense, it would seem that devotional leisure practice is by now defined 'by a multitude of individual acts of *self-identification*' (Bauman, 1992: 136). Sucked as it has been into the soft melt of liquid modern identity making, devotional leisure practice is but an individualized expression, painted only for individuals, which is also part of its liquid modernity. Outwardly it would appear that men and women are committed to their chosen devotional leisure practice, convinced that it is the motivational force in their lives, whereas in fact they are really dedicated to themselves. What this suggests is that individuals are too concerned with their own pleasure and happiness to accept any conscription to one devotional practice for any length of time – every leisure pursuit has to end at some point, in other words, but life goes on. What it suggests, too, is that it makes no difference *what* an individual will pick as his or her next devotional leisure practice, but as Heller (1999: 148) points out, it makes a difference *that* the person in question has freely picked it.

THE LABOUR OF LEISURE OR THE ART OF LIFE?

Whereas Rojek (2010) calls this kind of self-government the labour of leisure, Foucault (1984b) calls it the art of life. He suggested that a life freely chosen should use art; it is a necessity for an authentic life, not something to be admired for its aesthetic qualities. Art (and we would say leisure) should be plundered for new ideas about how to live – the 'art of life', as well as inspiration, moral lessons, comfort, and tales of the lives of others and how these might inform how we might live ourselves. Bauman (2008a) goes one step further than Foucault to suggest that the art of life is the way we all live now. In other words, because liquid modern men and women are free, they are always confronted with possibilities from among which they are obliged to choose, and in choosing, they are aware that they are denying all other possibilities except the one they have chosen. To embrace the art of life is to recognize one's individual freedom. Implicit to this is the recognition that individuals alone are responsible for their own lives; and that they can reach beyond who they are presently, because their identity, which is destined to remain forever incomplete, is a work in progress – one life, many identities. The choice to live one's life as a work of art indicates being prepared to reject the authority of former modes of existence; it also means being prepared to cope with the insecurity of a hitherto untried ontological status.

As Heller (1999) explains, these artists of life, all experts of one kind or another because of intensity of their passion, do not take on the legislating functions of solid modern hermeneutics. They do not present authentic leisure; they do not seek authority for their devotional practice. They do not even try to create a new tradition, for they do not stand in a continuous and strong tradition. True, they choose to join a devotional leisure practice, but because they are always on the verge of moving from one devotional leisure practice to another, it is merely shape-shifting that becomes the art of life. Men and women appear reluctant to want to embark on any one devotional leisure practice, because of the fear that to give oneself to one kind of life is to close down other opportunities, and, crucially, miss out on immediate pleasures. This new kind of devotion is more of a love affair with the self (and the body) rather than the leisure practice itself. This is another ambivalence of liquid leisure.

As Heller (p. 150) points out, the upshot of this is that hermeneutics is as a result removed from the continuity of its own tradition and devotional leisure practices become merely ephemeral points of attraction, which merely *feed* on tradition. It would appear that devotional leisure practice in liquid modernity is, as the philosopher James Carse (1986) would say, continued only for the purpose of continuing the play. What we fail to recognize, however, is that our individual desire to continue the play is only possible precisely because others go on with the game. What this means is that we forget that our entitlement to play must be counterbalanced with actively taking responsibility for the Other. The creedal currency of those shape-shifters who do choose to speak on behalf of the Other differs from that of the legislators, because they speak only in their own names, and draw back from pretending to speak in the name of authority. This is because, as Robinson (2009) argues, with a nod to the social capitalist Robert Putnam (2000), today they all choose to bowl alone, shop online, abandon cinemas for DVDs, and chat to each other electronically rather than go to a bar. In an increasingly self-centred society a premium is placed on being heard rather than listening, being seen rather than watching, and on being read rather than reading.

In other words, there is not much chance of the *skholē* tail wagging the imaginative leisure dog; the mode of 'expert' interpretation here is the cool attitude, which is hardly hermeneutics at all. It turns out that to call these liquid modern men and women interpreters is in itself misleading. For they do not really interpret at all. They are go-betweens rather than interpreters, or what Bourdieu calls the cultural intermediaries, those members of the new unrooted middle classes – postmodernity's ultra-cool set – who engage in the promotion and transmission of popular culture in order to legitimate devotional leisure practices as 'valid fields of intellectual analysis' (Featherstone, 1991). Bourdieu, like Heller, recognizes the gradual shift in the *modus operandi* of intellectual work, which sees the passing of the torch from traditional, legislating intellectuals to the intellectuals of a 'third culture' who shape the *Zeitgeist* by translating into 'objects of knowledge' the ostensible 'secrets' of devotional leisure practices into 'guide books' for living. Examples that fit this trend can be readily found in popular culture. For example, while the books written by Cass Pennant, ex-member and leader of the Inter City Firm football hooligan group associated with West Ham United in the 1970s have become prescribed reading for wannabe football hooligans, so the television programmes starring Gok Wan, such as *How to Look Good Naked* and *Gok's Fashion Fix*, have become essential watching for aspiring 'fashionistas'.

As Featherstone has forcefully argued, these cultural intermediaries have to some extent been effective in collapsing some of the most enduring distinctions and symbolic hierarchies between 'high' and 'low' cultures of taste and have been very successful in opening 'information channels between formerly sealed off areas of culture'. However, as Heller points out, because interpretations are presented as merely 'things that need to be known', these cultural intermediaries have little value beyond this largely self-absorbed communicative role, since they have effectively abandoned the vocation of hermeneutics. Ostensibly anyone can become a cultural intermediary, but this role is usually filled by the new leisure class – the celebrities – who have either found some fame in their chosen devotional leisure practice or have brought fame to it.

We might all be artists of life these days but we seem to have forgotten what the true meaning and purpose of hermeneutics is about. As Heller (2005) points out, hermeneutics is the basis of truth in the modern world since freedom itself is entirely unfit to serve this type of function, because it is based on a foundation that cannot found; this is because modernity is always in the process of reinventing itself. It is in this process that the interpretive substance of hermeneutics seems to have been left behind by the world. As we have seen, however, liquid modernity is a world of infinite interpretability and choice of devotional leisure practices is not going to dry up anytime in the near future. What the foregoing discussion suggests, though, is that in giving up the true vocation of hermeneutics (read: *skholê*) we not only seem to have lost interest in trying to find out leisure's secret, but we also seem to have given up on trying to find out the secret to ourselves, the key to the art of life proper.

LEISURE AND THE ART OF LIFE

Perhaps the greatest virtue of leisure is that it allows us to suspend for the time being the weight of the world, to be irresponsible and delight in it, the way that children do when they play. As we saw in the last chapter, even in consumer leisure activities underpinned by IKEAization, there is this creativity of action. But what is missing when the consumer attitude dominates our leisure is that the *necessity* of consuming replaces the *contingency* of play, and the rules that govern the performativity criterion take over. In other words, consuming not only stands for the quick absorption of pleasure and fleeting happiness, rather the slow burn of delight of experiencing the same kinds of feeling over a longer period of time, but what we also lack is the deepest conviction that the freedom that allows us to experience our chosen devotional leisure practice has been hard won. This makes our leisure more serious than we know. What liquid modern men and women fail to recognize is that it is precisely because we are free that we have the power to look directly into the centre of our chosen devotional leisure practice the way only children can, and with this capability to imagine things anew.

What this would seem to suggest is that we lack some rules of leisure for the games we play so freely, and only by making some new rules will we be able to take the responsibility *for* responsibility that freedom brings. The trouble is that in a free world 'new rules of leisure' cannot be set out in advance, because to do so would be to undermine the ambivalence that is the basis of leisure. But what is ambivalence? I am not using the concept here simplistically to mean that all things have their good and bad aspects, i.e. serious leisure is good leisure, casual leisure is bad leisure. I am using ambivalence in its central meaning: 'the achievement of a goal with the realization that the *struggle*, not the goal itself, was what we perhaps really wanted' (von Weizäcker, 1988: 65). In other words, it is the realization of the human imagination with the insight that it was the chase, not leisure as an end in itself, that we really wanted. To borrow an analogy from Bauman, what we really crave is to chase the hare, not to catch it. The pleasure is in hunting, not in catching the prey.

What this suggests to me is that what we should be doing instead of finding some 'new rules of leisure' is finding new ways for making our leisure more meaningful. In other words, using hermeneutics to inform the art of life in new ways that are rich and surprising to rekindle our interest in finding out its secret, which as we have just seen is a project which is forever unfinished, perhaps unfinishable. As Heller points out, good interpretation deepens words and makes them more meaningful, creating its own democratic operating principles as it proceeds. To this extent, hermeneutics makes different ways of experiencing leisure possible. And not only that, if we engage in hermeneutics, we also have the potential to transform *individual* contingency into *collective* destiny; and we might even make a better world possible.

What this also suggests is that another kind of life is possible. As we have seen, the liquid modern present day world we inhabit is a starting over world, a world forever in embryo, and the best, the most human thing that we should all learn by heart is that if this means our lives are inevitably governed by contingency rather than fixity, and ambivalence rather than certainty, and that if all of this weighs heavy on our individual shoulders, it also presents us with the opportunity for perpetual renewal and the concomitant changeability of reality, which can only mean, as Hannah Arendt would have been pleased to observe, the arrival of new beings 'who would, or could, say and do things no one had said or done before' and who 'might move others to speak and act in new ways as well' (Robin, 2007). What we need to do in our lives is get away from the re-usable language found in the consumer world to generate new cultural discourses that are able to speak for the first time. Instead of greedily consuming one devotional practice after another, we need to get greedy for the small, true details of life that leisure offers us. It is only when we are able to grasp this possibility that we will be able step clear of consumer cluttered lives into a new relationship with ourselves and the world, one which is at once simpler and more profound than the liquid life pursued under what current conditions allow.

It would seem from what I have said already that the art of life is intractably an individual concern and that it is destined to reflect the cool attitude that prevails in liquid modernity. However, once an individual recognizes the fact that she can live an autonomous and authentic life, she also recognizes that as an individual herself is the foundation of all values – to reiterate, as Agnes Heller (2005) points out, freedom itself is entirely unfit to serve this function because it is a foundation that cannot found – which also means that she is inseparable from all others, because her free choice of values determines the conditions under which others themselves choose. It is on this basis of interdependent responsibility for the self and the Other that the art of living prospers as a universalizable ethical mode of existence. It is through the art of living that the individual has the *potential* to be his or her own completed self, nothing less than an individual world – each individual separate and unique but still bound to one another through the felt presence of their shared humanity. This raises an important question, 'What is it that provides the basis of such an honourable framework for living one's life?'

'Nietzsche once said that it is easy to dance in chains', explains Heller (1999: 150), but 'it is more difficult to dance after having been liberated of chains'. In other words, since freedom imposes no constraints on us, to find it we need to impose some kind of constraints on ourselves. This is the world revealed by *skholē,* which provides the kind of standards and values we need if we are to do anything better than shape-shift. To tweak the honourable framework set out by Nietzsche:

> For what is called the art of life is always a self-imposed constraint. 'Dancing in chains' making it difficult for oneself when spreading over it the illusion of ease – that is the artifice that we all must learn. Already in the world there exists an abundance of inherited choreography with which we might learn to dance; and with which we might learn to create new dance routines for those coming after us. These inherited conventions will never speak to us, however, unless we take time to listen in leisure, because they speak only in an educated voice that is too knowledgeable and cultured to be merely consumed. This is *skholē,* the educated-school of the poets, the artists of life: firstly to let a manifold constraint be imposed on oneself through the conventions of earlier poets; so as then to invent a new constraint, to impose

it on oneself and conquer it gracefully: so that constraint and its defeat become known and admired.

(cited in Dudley, 2002: 221)

Truth is encountered and demonstrated in our leisure – even in IKEA leisure. However, without *skholē* (read: hermeneutics) we are unlikely to learn how to use our leisure wisely. This is the important message emanating from Rojek's (2010) thesis in *The Labour of Leisure*. Northrop Frye (1963) argues that the only exceptions to this rule, and they are exceptions that prove the rule, are those individuals who, when confronted with losing their own chance to set themselves free, show that they have an imagination strong and advanced enough to offer an alternative vision. In the world of solid modernity when freedom still had to be fought for and constraints didn't have to be self-fashioned, the world had to rely on these authentic poets.

Zygmunt Bauman was born into a Jewish family in Poznan, Poland in 1925, survived the Second World War, but was forced to leave his country of birth in an anti-Semitic purge. He eventually made a new home in Leeds. Similarly, Agnes Heller was forced to leave her home in Budapest, Hungary because of her political beliefs, especially her objections to the Soviet invasion of Czechoslovakia in 1968 (Auer in Heller and Auer, 2009), to take a teaching post at La Trobe University in Melbourne, Australia. However, their exile provided both of these intellectuals, who between them have provided most of the scholarship that forms the basis of this book, with an opportunity to reflect properly on the life that they had already had, as well as the state of the world in which they had lived in, in both cases a Cold War communist world. As a result both realized in their own individual ways that their own individual lives had consisted of all sorts of contingent events, and once they each started to put all of these things together managed to become not just someone or other, but themselves. In other words, authentic poets who had not only discovered what it means to be unified and happy in themselves as individuals, but who had also gained a clear sense of the historical contingency of their own individual fates (and the fates of others like them), and who as a result, to paraphrase Heller, were both able to grasp the point that life does not serve any purpose higher than being lived. In this process both had also become autonomous and moral individuals, who, like Foucault (1984: 350) could ask themselves the question: 'Why should the lamp or the house be an art object, but not my life?'

CONCLUSION

He doesn't use the term, but what Foucault is getting at when he asks this question is that if the everyday world we reside in and the imaginative play world of leisure – that experimental world where we are always engaging with the thrill of the search for something and the exhilaration of discovery – are different worlds, the imaginative play world of leisure is more important. What this would appear to suggest is that Rojek is right after all. Without *skholē* (read: hermeneutics) we don't have any proper means of validating that kind of leisure that feels like it is our fate, our reason for living, of giving life its true meaning and purpose by turning the human imagination into reality. What he seems reluctant to acknowledge, however, is that, for some people, leisure is also the antithesis of work, sometimes work itself, rest, idleness, having a good time, a bit of fun, and much else besides, which it should be repeated, is *not* the same thing as *skholē*, but it is leisure all the same.

In the last chapter, we also saw that Rojek has a tendency to underestimate individuality of men and women he supposes are in thrall of consumerism, while simultaneously overestimating the grip of modern 'iron cage' rationalization systems. There is no doubt that for many people today the meaning of leisure inevitably seems to lie in the unalloyed pleasure and happiness they find in consuming. But perhaps in their leisure pursuits it is not consuming that they are really after at all, but the pursuit of life itself – its highs and lows, frustrations and disappointments, the inevitable mixture of partial successes and unfulfilled dreams – and that is what really counts. What this suggests to me is that the meaning of life is the meaning of leisure, and even if it remains elusive, it presents us with myriad opportunities to grab hold of intimations of the absolute. Rojek is wrong. Freedom is not just for the birds.

CONCLUSIONS

In an edited collection of his work *Philosophical Occasions, 1912–1951* (1993) Wittgenstein observes that philosophy often leads us into seemingly fruit-less confusion. We ask questions that sound sensible, answerable ques-tions, but they often turn out to be nothing of the sort. In explaining how this works he says that philosophers habitually behave like children who jot some random lines on a piece of paper and then ask an adult 'What is that?' Wittgenstein explains that this kind of thing usually happens in the following way: the adult had drawn some pictures for the child several times and said 'This is a house', 'This is mummy', 'This is a dog' and so on. And then the child makes some marks on a piece of paper too and asks the adult 'What is this then?'

What Wittgenstein is describing here is what we have been doing in this book, and hopefully to good effect. With a bit of luck it happened like this. We built up a picture of leisure out of an array of different words, and we found out that each of these stood for something. Our picture of leisure also contained some things, not necessarily words, that could not be deciphered, such as leisure's secret, its *unknown known*. We also found out that much of what we call leisure occupies an ineffable space in between words, loaded with contradictions, even when the words clearly appear to mean something specific; the space between work and leisure, for example. These words ought to stand for something clear. You can actually see the function that they perform. But when you ask the ques-tion: 'What is this then?', there is no definitive answer. The words will not read. What I am describing here is the language game of leisure as it is played by leisure scholars.

We have also been playing the same language game. This is how we have followed Wittgenstein's invitation and embarked on the educational journey of *skholē* that is this book. What we should have learnt at the end of this journey is that we should stop asking after the meaning and purpose of leisure and ask after its use instead. To modify what Agnes Heller (2009: 8) said about another topic, we should have also learnt to never again try to answer the question 'What is Leisure?' since this question is unanswerable or all that has ever been written about leisure is in fact the only answer to this question. Whether it is the first answer or the second does not really matter, because they amount to the same thing.

REFERENCES

Abrams, P. (1982) *Historical Sociology*. Shepton Mallet: Open Books.

Adorno, T.W. and Horkheimer, M. (1944) 'The Culture Industry: The Enlightenment of Mass Deception', in T. W. Adorno and M. Horkheimer (eds) *Dialectic of Enlightenment*. http://ad3.wdfiles.com/local – files/start/Adorno.pdf on 16th May 2009.

Aitchison, C.C. (2003) *Gender and Leisure: Social and Cultural Perspectives*. London: Routledge.

Alfino, M., Caputo, J. and Wynyard, R. (eds) (1998) *McDonaldization Revisited*. Westport, CT: Greenwood Press.

Anderson, B. (1991) *Imagined Communities: Reflections on the Origin and Spread of Nationalism*. Second Edition. London: Verso.

Atkinson, M. (2002) 'Fifty Million Viewers Can't Be Wrong: Professional Wrestling, Sports Entertainment, and Mimesis', *Sociology of Sport Journal*, 19 (1): 47–66.

Auge, M. (1995) *Non-Places: Introduction to an Anthropology of Supermodernity*. Translated by John Howe. London: Verso.

Austin, J.L. (1962) *How to Do Things with Words*. Edited by J.O. Urmson and M. Sbisa. Cambridge, MA: Harvard University Press.

Bachelard, G. (1994 1964) *The Poetics of Space*. Boston: Beacon Press.

Back, L., Crabbe, T. and Solomos, J. (2001) *The Changing Face of Football: Racism, Identity and Multiculture in the English Game*. Oxford: Berg.

Bailey, P.C. (1978) *Leisure and Class in Victorian England: Rational Recreation and the Contest for Control, 1830–1885*. London: Routledge.

—— (1989) 'Leisure, Culture and the Historian: Reviewing the First Generation of Leisure Historiography in Britain', *Leisure Studies*, 8, 107–27.

Bailly, O., Caudron, J-M. and Lambart, D. (2006) 'Secret Hidden Behind IKEA's Wardrobes', *Le Monde Diplomatique*, December.

Ball, S. J. (2003) 'It's Not What You Know: Education and Social Capital', *Sociology Review*, November.

Baudrillard, J. (1970) *The Consumer Society*. London: Sage.

—— (1981) *For A Critique of the Political Economy of the Sign*: St Louis, MI: Telos.

—— (1989) *America*. London: Verso.

—— (1990 1983) *Fatal Strategies*. London: Pluto.

—— (1998) *Paroxysm: Interviews with Phillipe Petit*. London: Verso.

—— (2001) *Impossible Exchange*. London: Verso.

Bauman, Z. (1987) *Legislators and Interpreters: On Modernity, Post-Modernity and Intellectuals*. Cambridge: Polity Press.

—— (1988) *Freedom*. Buckingham: Open University Press.

—— (1990) *Thinking Sociologically*. Oxford: Blackwell.

—— (1991) *Modernity and Ambivalence*. Cambridge: Polity Press.

—— (1992) *Intimations of Postmodernity*. London: Routledge.

—— (1994) 'Is there a Postmodern Sociology?', in S. Seidman *The Postmodern Turn*. Cambridge: Cambridge University Press.

—— (1997) *Postmodernity and its Discontents*. Cambridge: Polity Press.

—— (1998) *Work, Consumerism and the New Poor*. Buckingham: Open University Press.

—— (1999a) *In Search of Politics*. Cambridge, Polity Press.

—— (1999b) *Culture as Praxis*. London: Sage.

—— (2000a) *Liquid Modernity*. Cambridge: Polity Press.

—— (2000b) 'Book Review of the McDonaldization Thesis: Explorations and Extensions by George Ritzer', *Journal of Contigencies and Crisis Management*, 8(4): p. 234.

—— (2001) *Community: Seeking Safety in an Insecure World*. Cambridge: Polity Press.

—— (2004) *Identity: Conversations with Benedetto Vecchi*. Cambridge: Polity Press.

—— (2006) *Liquid Fear*. Cambridge: Polity Press.

—— (2007) *Consuming Life*. Cambridge: Polity Press.

—— (2008a) *The Art of Life*. Cambridge: Polity Press.

—— (2008b) *Does Ethics Have a Chance in a World of Consumers?* Cambridge (Massachusetts) and London: Harvard University Press.

Beck, U. (2002) 'Zombie Categories: Interview with Ulrich Beck', in U. Beck and E. Beck-Gernsheim, *Individualization: Institutionalized Individualism and its Social and Political Consequences*. London: Sage.

Becker, H.S. (1963) *Outsiders: Studies in the Sociology of Deviance*. London: The Free Press.

Beilharz, P. (2000) *Zygmunt Bauman: Dialectic of Modernity*. London: Sage.

Bell, D. (1973) *The Coming of Post-Industrial Society*. New York: Basic Books.

Black, T. (2009) '"We Want to Determine the World, Not be Determined by It": An Interview with Susan Neiman'. http://www.spiked-online.com/ on 12th August 2009.

Blackshaw, T. (2002) 'Interview With Zygmunt Bauman', *Network: Newsletter of the British Sociological Association*, 83, October.

—— (2003) *Leisure Life: Myth Masculinity and Modernity*. London: Routledge.

—— (2005) *Zygmunt Bauman*. Abingdon: Routledge.

—— (2008) 'Contemporary Community Theory and Football', *Soccer and Society*, 9(3): 325–45.

—— (2009a) 'Introduction', in T. Blackshaw and G. Crawford, *The Sage Dictionary of Leisure Studies*. London: Sage.

—— (2009b) *Key Concepts in Community Studies*. London: Sage.

—— and Crabbe, T. (2004) *New Perspectives on Sport and 'Deviance': Consumption, Performativity and Social Control*. Abingdon: Routledge.

—— and Crabbe, T. (2005) 'Leeds on Trial: Soap Opera, Performativity and the Racialization of Sports-Related Violence', *Patterns of Prejudice*, 39, (3): 327–42.

—— and Crawford, G. (2009) *The Sage Dictionary of Leisure Studies*. London: Sage.

—— and Long, J. (2005) 'What's the Big Idea? A Critical Exploration of the Concept of Social Capital and its Incorporation into Leisure Policy Discourse', *Leisure Studies*, 24(3): 239–58.

Borsay, P. (2006) *A History of Leisure: The British Experience since 1500*. Basingstoke: Macmillan.

Bourdieu, P. (1984) *Distinction: A Social Critique of the Judgment of Taste*. London: Routledge

—— (1999) *The Weight of the World: Social Suffering in Contemporary Society*. Cambridge: Polity Press.

—— (2000) *Pascalian Meditations*. Cambridge: Polity Press.

—— and Wacquant, L. (1992) *An Invitation to Reflexive Sociology*. Cambridge: Polity Press.

Brackenridge, C.H. (1994) 'Fair Play or Fair Game: Child Sexual Abuse in Sport Organisations', *International Review for the Sociology of Sport*, 29 (3): 287–99.

Brackenridge, C. (2001) *Spoilsports: Understanding and Preventing Sexual Exploitation in Sports*. London: Routledge.

—— and Fasting, K. (eds) (2002) *Sexual Harassment and Abuse in Sport: International Research and Policy Perspectives*. London: Whiting and Birch.

Bramham, P. (2002) 'Rojek, the Sociological Imagination and Leisure', *Leisure Studies*, 21 (3/4): 221–34.

—— (2006) 'Hard and Disappearing Work: Making Sense of the Leisure Project', *Leisure Studies*, 25 (40): 379–90.

Bray, E. (2009) 'The New Link between Music and Fashion', *The Independent*, 21st August.

Breivik, G. (ed.). (1999) *Empirical Studies of Risk Sports*. Oslo: Norges idrett-shøgskole; Institutt for Sammfunnsfag.

Brohm, J-M. (1978) *Sport: A Prison of Measured Time*. London: Ink Links Ltd.

Brown, A., Crabbe, T. and Mellor, G. (2008) 'FC United of Manchester: Supporter Communities and Contesting Corporate Football', in A.

Brown, T. Crabbe and G. Mellor (eds) *Football and Community in the Global Context: Studies in Theory and Practice*. Abingdon: Routledge.

Caillois, R. (1961) *Man, Play and Games*. London: Thames & Hudson.

Carpenter, R. (1976) *Thomas Hardy*. London: The Macmillan Press Ltd.

Carse, J.P. (1986) *Finite and Infinite Games: A Vision of Life as Play and Possibility*. New York: Ballantine.

—— (2008) *The Religious Case Against Belief*. London: Penguin.

Clarke, J. and Critcher, C. (1985) *The Devil Makes Work*. London: Macmillan.

Coetzee, J. M. (2009a) '"Summertime": Undated Fragments', *New York Review of Books*, 56 (12): 16th July.

—— (2009b) '"Summertime": Notebooks 1972–75', *New York Review of Books*, 56 (13): 13th August.

Conrad, P. (2006) 'The Making of the Girl Next Door', *Observer Review*, 3rd December.

Coward, B. (2003) *The Stuart Age: England 1603–1714*. Third Edition. London: Longman.

Critcher, C. (1989) 'A Communication in Response to Leisure, Lifestyle and Status: A Pluralist Framework for Analysis', *Leisure Studies*, 8(2): 159–62.

—— and Bramham, P. (2004) 'The Devil Still Makes Work', in J.T. Haworth and A.J. Veal (eds) *Work and Leisure*. London: Routledge.

Csikszentmihalyi, M. (1974) *Flow: Studies of Enjoyment*. Chicago: University of Chicago Press.

—— (1990) *Flow: The Psychology of Optimal Experience*. New York: HarperPerennial.

—— (1997) *Living Well: The Psychology of Everyday Life*. London: Weidenfeld Nicholson.

Cummings, D. (2009) 'There is more to Calvin than Dourness and Asceticism', *Spiked Online*. http://www.spiked-online.com/index.php/site/article/7264 on 14th August.

Cunningham, H. (1980) *Leisure in the Industrial Revolution c.1780–1880*, London: Croom Helm.

Debord. G. (1995 1967) *The Society of the Spectacle*. New York: Zone Books.

Deem, R. (1986) *All Work and No Play?* Milton Keynes: Open University Press.

Dennis, K. and Urry, J. (2009) *After the Car*. Cambridge: Polity Press.

Diski, J. (2009) 'All Eat All', *London Review of Books*, 31 (15): 8th August.

Downes, D. and Rock, P. (1998) *Understanding Deviance: A guide to the Sociology of Crime and Rule Breaking*. Oxford: Oxford Univeristy Press.

Dudley, W. (2002) *Hegel, Nietzsche and Philosophy: Thinking Freedom*. Cambridge: Cambridge University Press.

Dumazedier, J. (1974) 'Leisure and the Social System', in J.F. Murphy (ed.) *Concepts of Leisure*. Englewood Cliffs, NJ: Prentice-Hall.

Dunning, E. (1999) *Sport Matters: Sociological Studies of Sport, Violence and Civilization*. London: Routledge.

Eagleton, T. (2005) 'Lend Me a Fiver', *London Review of Books*, 27 (12): 23rd June.

—— (2007) *The Meaning of Life*. Oxford: Oxford University Press.

Eco, U. (1985) quoted in P. French (2006) 'Watch This Movie or Die', *The Observer Review*, 1st October.

Elias, N. (1991 1939) *The Society of Individuals*. Oxford: Blackwell.

—— (1994) *The Civilizing Process: The History of Manners and State-Formation and Civilization*. Integrated Edition. Oxford: Blackwell.

—— and Dunning, E. (1986) (eds) *Quest for Excitement: Sport and Leisure in the Civilizing Process*. Oxford: Basil Blackwell.

Elton, G.R. (1963) *Reformation Europe*. London: Fontana.

Ehrenreich, B. (2007) *Dancing in the Streets: A History of Collective Joy*. London: Granta.

Featherstone, M. (1991) *Consumer Culture and Postmodernism*. London: Sage.

Feeley, M. and Simon, J. (1992) 'The New Penology: Notes on the Emerging Strategy of Corrections and its Implications', *Criminology*, 30 (4): 449–74.

Ferguson, H. (1989) 'Sigmund Freud and the Pursuit of Pleasure', in C. Rojek (ed.) *Leisure for Leisure: Critical Essays*. Basingstoke: Macmillan.

—— (2009) *Self-Identity and Everyday Life*. London: Routledge.

Foucault, M. (1979) *The History of Sexuality: Volume 1: An Introduction*. Harmondsworth: Pelican.

—— (1984a) 'Of Other Spaces (1967), Heterotopias'. Translated by Jay Miskowiec. http://foucault.info/documents/heteroTopia/foucault.heteroTopia.en.html on 12th October, 2008.

—— (1984b): 'On Genealogy of Ethics: An Overview of Work in Progress', in P. Rabinow (ed.) *The Foucault Reader: An Introduction to Foucault's Thought*. Harmondsworth: Penguin.

—— (1986) *The Order of Things: An Archaeology of the Human Sciences*. London: Routledge.

—— (2009) *Self-Identity and Everyday Life*. Abingdon: Routledge.

French, P. (2006) 'What this Movie of Die', *Observer Review*, 1st October.

Freud, S. (1950) *Beyond the Pleasure Principle*. A new translation by James Strachey. London: Hogarth Press.

Frugoni, C. (2005) *A Day in a Medieval City*. Chicago: Chicago University Press.

Frye, N. (1963) *The Educated Imagination*. Toronto: Canadian Broadcasting Corporation.

Fulgham, R. (1995) *From Beginning to End*. New York: Ballantine Books.

Garnett, M. and Weight, R. (2004) *Modern British History: The Essential A–Z Guide*. London: Pimlico.

Gellner, E.A. (1964) *Thought and Change*. London: Weidenfeld and Nicolson.

George, C.H. and George, K. (1961) *The Protestant Mind of English Reformation*. London: Methuen.

Giddens, A. (1976) 'Introduction', M. Weber (1930) *The Protestant Ethic and the Spirit of Capitalism*. London: Unwin Hyman Ltd.

—— (1984) *The Constitution of Society*. Cambridge: Polity Press.

—— (1994) 'Living in Post-Traditional Society', in U. Beck, A. Giddens and S. Lash, *Reflexive Modernization: Politics, Tradition and Aesthetics in the Modern Social Order*. Cambridge: Polity Press.

Glennie, P and Thrift, N. (1996) 'Reworking E.P. Thompson's Time, Work Discipline and Industrial Capitalism', *Time and Society*, 5 (3): 275–99.

—— (2009) *Shaping the Day: A History of Timekeeping in England and Wales 1300–1800*. Oxford: Oxford University Press.

Glyptis, S. (1989) *Leisure and Unemployment*. Milton Keynes: Open University Press.

Grayling, A.C. (2000) 'The Last Word On ... Leisure', *The Guardian*, 5th Februrary.

Green, E. (1998) '"Women Doing Friendship": An Analysis of Women's Leisure as a Site of Identity, Empowerment and Resistance', *Leisure Studies*, 17, 171–85.

——, Hebron, S. and Woodward, D. (1990) *Women's Leisure, What Leisure?* London: Macmillan.

Green, R.W. (1959) *Protestantism and Capitalism: The Weber Thesis and its Critics*. Boston: Heath and Company.

Habermas, J. (1976) *Legitimation Crisis*. London: Heinemann Educational Books.

—— (1987) *The Theory of Communicative Action*. Beacon: Boston.

Harland, R. (1987) *Superstructuralism: The Philosophy of Structuralism and Post-Structuralism*. London: Routledge.

Harris, D. (2005) *Key Concepts in Leisure Studies*. London: Sage.

Harris, J. (2009) 'Don't Look Back', *The Guardian*, 27th June.

Harvey, D. (1989) *The Condition of Postmodernity*. Oxford: Blackwell.

Haywood, L., Kew, F., Bramham, P., Spink, J., Capenerhurst, J. and Henry, I. (1995) *Understanding Leisure*. Second Edition. Cheltenham: Stanley Thornes.

Heller, A. (1992) 'World, Things, Life and Home', *Thesis Eleven*, 33 (1): 69–84.

—— (1998) 'Interviews with Agnes Heller'. http://homepage.ntlworld.com/simon.tormey/articles/hellerinterview.html on 12th November, 2008.

—— (1999) *A Theory of Modernity*. Oxford: Blackwell.

—— (2005) 'The Three Logics of Modernity and the Double Bind of the Modern Imagination', *Thesis Eleven*, 81 (1): 63–79.

—— (2009) *A Theory of Feelings*. Second Edition. Plymouth: Lexington Books.

—— and Auer, S. (2009) 'An Interview with Agnes Heller', *Thesis Eleven*, 97 (2): 99–105.

Hoberman, J. (1997) *Darwin's Athletes: How Sport Damaged Black America and Preserved the Myth of Race*. Boston: Houghton Mifflin.

Hobsbawm, E. (1995) *Age of Extremes: The Short Twentieth Century 1914–1991*. London: Abacus.

Hoggart, R. (1966 1957) *The Uses of Literacy*. Harmondsworth: Pelican.

—— (1973) *Speaking to Each Other. Volume One: About Society*. Harmondsworth: Penguin.

Honneth, A. 'An Interview with Axel Honneth: The Role of Sociology in the Theory of Recognition'. Interviewed by Anders Peterson and Rasmus Willig. *European Journal of Social Theory*, 5(2): 265–77.

Hoppen, K. T. (1998) *The Mid-Victorian Generation 1846–1886*. Oxford: Oxford University Press.

Hornsey, R. (2006) 'Join the Club', *London Review of Books*, 28 (17): 28th September.

Horrocks, C. (1999) *Baudrillard and the Millennium*. New York: Icon Books.

Houlbrook, M. (2005) *Queer London: Perils and Pleasures in the Sexual Metropolis, 1918–1957*. London: University of Chicago Press.

Huizinga, J. (1955) *Homo Ludens: A Study of the Play-Element in Culture*. Boston: Beacon Press.

Jameson, F. (1991) *Postmodernism, or, The Cultural Logic of Late Capitalism*. London: Verso.

Jones, J. (2007) 'Beyond Lust', in *The Guardian*, 16th October.

Kalfus, K. (2006) *A Disorder Peculiar to the Country*. London: Simon and Schuster.

Kane, P. (2004) *Play Ethic: A Manifesto for a Different Way of Living*. Basingstoke: Macmillan.

—— (2006) 'The Power of Play', *Soundings (Summer)*.

Kaplan, M. (1975) *Leisure: Theory and Practice*. New York: John Wiley.

Katz, J. (1988) *Seductions of Crime*. New York: Basic Books.

Kynaston, D. (2007) *Austerity Britain 1945–51*. London: Bloomsbury.

Lane, J.F. (2000) *Pierre Bourdieu: A Critical Introduction*. London: Pluto Press.

Lash, S. (2002a) *Critique of Information*. London: Sage.

—— (2002b) 'Foreword: Individualization in No-Linear Mode', in U. Beck and E. Beck-Gernsheim, *Individualization*. London: Sage.

Laviolette, P. (2006) 'Green and Extreme: Free-flowing Through Seascape and Sewer', *WorldViews: Environment, Culture, Religion*, 10 (2): 178–204.

Le Breton, D. (2000) 'Playing Symbolically with Death in Extreme Sports', *Body & Society*, 6 (1): 1–11.

Levitas, R. (1998) *The Inclusive Society: Social Exclusion and New Labour*. Basingstoke: Macmillan.

Lianos, M. with Douglas, M. (2000) 'Dangerization and the End of Deviance: The Institutional Environment', in D. Garland and R. Sparks (eds) *Criminology and Social Theory*. Oxford: Oxford University Press.

Loy, J.W., McPherson, B.D. and Kenyon, G. (1978) *Sport and the Social System*. Reading, MA: Addison-Wesley.

Lundberg, G. A., Komarovski, M. and McInnery, M.A. (1934) *Leisure: A Suburban Study*. New York: Columbia University Press.

Lyng, S. (1990) 'Edgework: A Social Psychological Analysis of Voluntary Risk Taking', *American Journal of Sociology*, 95(4): 851–86.

—— (2005) (ed.) *Edgework: The Sociology of Risk-Taking*. Abingdon: Routledge.

Lyotard, J-F. (1984 1979) *The Postmodern Condition: A Report on Knowledge*. Minneapolis, MN: University of Minnesota Press.

Maffesoli, M. (1996) *The Time of the Tribes: The Decline of Individualism in a Mass Society*. London: Sage.

Malcolmson, R. (1973) *Popular Recreations in English Society, 1700–1850*. Cambridge: Cambridge University Press.

Marwick, A. (1998) *The Sixties*. Oxford: Oxford University Press.

Maslow, A. (1968) *Toward a Psychology of Being*. Princeton, NJ: D. Van Nostrand Co.

Merton, R.K. (1973) *The Sociology of Science: Theoretical and Empirical Investigations*. Chicago: Chicago University Press.

Mills, C.W. (1959) *The Sociological Imagination*. New York: Harper and Row.

Milton, J. (1968) *Paradise Lost and Paradise Regained*. New York: Airmont.

Morgan, W. (1994) *Leftist Theories of Sport*. Urbana, IL: University of Illinois Press.

Nehamas, A. (1998) *The Art of Living: Socratic Reflections from Plato to Foucault*. London: University of California Press.

Neulinger, J. (1974) *The Psychology of Leisure*. Springfield, IL: Charles C. Thomas.

Nietzsche, F. (1977) *A Nietzsche Reader*. Selected and Translated with an Introduction by R.J. Hollingdale. Harmondsworth: Penguin.

Oates, J. C. (2008) 'In the Rough Country', *New York Review of Books*, 55 (16): 23rd October.

O'Connor, R. (2009) 'Pubs Closing at a Rate of 52 a Week as Hard-up Drinkers Shun their Local', *The Times*, 22nd July.

O'Hagan, A. (2009) 'A Car of One's Own', in *London Review of Books*, 31 (11): 11th June.

Olivier, S. (2006) 'Moral Dilemmas of Participation in Dangerous Leisure Activities', *Leisure Studies*, 25 (1): 95–109.

Pamuk, O. (2005) 'As Others See Us', *The Guardian*, 29th October.

Parker, S. (1971) *The Future of Work and Leisure*. London: McGibbon Kee.

—— (1983) *Leisure and Work*. London: George Allen and Unwyn.

Phillips, A. (2003) 'Bored With Sex', *London Review of Books*, 25 (5): 6th March.

Pieper, J. (1998 1948) *Leisure: The Basis of Culture*. South Bend, IN: St. Augustine's Press.

Plumb, J.H. (1973) *The Commercialization of Leisure in Eighteenth Century England*. Reading: University of Reading Press.

Poder, P. (2007) 'Relatively Liquid Interpersonal Relationships in Flexible Work Life', in Anthony Elliott (ed.) *The Contemporary Bauman*. Abingdon: Routledge.

Poster, M. (1994) 'Critical Theory and Technoculture: Habermas and Baudrillard', in D. Kellner (ed.) *Baudrillard: A Critical Reader*. Oxford: Blackwell.

Potolsky, M. (2006) *Mimesis*. Abingdon: Routledge.

Putnam, R.D. (2000) Bowling Alone: The Collapse and Revival of American Community. New York: Simon & Schuster.

Rancière, J. (2008) 'Jacques Rancière and Indisciplinarity: An Interview with Marie-Aude Baronian and Mireille Rosello', posted on *Void Manufacturing*. http://voidmanufacturing.wordpress.com/2008/10/15/jacques-ranciere-interview-2007/ on 15th October.

Ridge, D.T. (2004) '"It was an Incredible Thrill": The Social Meanings and Dynamics of Younger Gay Men's Experiences of Barebacking in Melbourne', *Sexualities*, 7 (3): 259–79.

Ritzer, G. (1993) *The McDonaldization of Society*. Newbury Park: Pine Forge Press.

—— (1998) *The McDonaldization Thesis: Explorations and Extensions*. London: Sage.

—— (2003) *Contemporary Social theory and Its Classical Roots: The Basics*. New York: McGraw Hill.

—— (2004) *The Globalization of Nothing*. London: Pine Forge Press.

Roberts, K. (1970) *Leisure*. London: Longman.

—— (1978) *Contemporary Society and the Growth of Leisure*. London: Longman.

—— (1981) *Leisure*. Second Edition. London: Longman.

—— (1983) *Youth and Leisure*. London: Allen & Unwin.

—— (1999) *Leisure in Contemporary Society*. Wallingford: CABI.

Robin, C. (2007) 'Dragon-Slayers', *London Review of Books*, 29 (1): 4th January.

Robinson, C. (2009) 'Diary', *London Review of Books*, 36: 26th February.

Robinson, D.W. (1992) 'A Descriptive Model of Enduring Risk Recreation Involvement', *Journal of Leisure Research*, 24 (1): 52–63.

Robinson, K. (2003) 'The Passion and the Pleasure Foucault's Art of Not Being Oneself', *Theory, Culture and Society*, 20 (2): 119–44.

Rogers, C. (1961) *On Becoming a Person: A Therapist's View of Psychotherapy*. London: Constable.

Rojek, C. (1985) *Capitalism and Leisure Theory*. London: Tavistock.

—— (1990) 'Baudrillard and Leisure', *Leisure Studies*, 9 (1): 7–20.

—— (1995) *Decentring Leisure: Rethinking Leisure Theory*. London: Sage.

—— (2000) *Leisure and Culture*. Basingstoke: Macmillan.

—— (2004) 'The Consumerist Syndrome in Contemporary Society: An Interview with Zygmunt Bauman', *Journal of Consumer Culture*, 4 (3): 291–312.

—— (2005) *Leisure Theory: Principles and Practice*. Basingstoke: Palgrave Macmillan.

—— (2010) *The Labour of Leisure: The Culture of Free Time*. London: Sage.

Rorty, R. (2007) *Philosophy and Cultural Politics: Philosophical Papers*. Cambridge: Cambridge University Press.

Rose, N. (1999) *Powers of Freedom: Reframing Political Thought*. Cambridge: Cambridge University Press.

Rutherford, J. (2007) *After Identity*. London: Lawrence and Wishart.

Samuelsson, K. (1961) *Religion and Economic Action*. London: Routledge and Kegan Paul.

Sassoon, D. (2005) 'From Buddenbrooks to Babbitt?', *New Left Review*, 36: 141–8.

Scraton, S. and Bramham, P. (1995) 'Leisure and Postmodernity', in M. Haralambos (ed.) *Developments in Sociology Volume 11*. Ormskirk: Causeway Press.

Scruton, R. (1998) 'Introduction', in J. Pieper, *Leisure: The Basis of Culture*. South Bend, IN: St. Augustine's Press.

—— (2008) 'Review of The Craftsman by Richard Sennett', *The Sunday Times*, 10th February.

—— (2009) 'In Vino Veritas: I'll Drink to That', *Standpoint Online*, June.

Seabrook J. (1988) *The Leisure Society*. London: Blackwell.

Sennett, Richard (1977) *The Fall of Public Man: On the Social Psychology of Capitalism*. New York: Alfred A. Knopf.

—— (2003) *Respect: The Formation of Character in an Age of Inequality*. London: Allen Lane.

—— (2005) *The Culture of the New Capitalism: Castle Lectures in Ethics, Politics, and Economics*. New York: Yale.

—— (2008) 'Labours of Love', in *The Guardian*, 2nd February.

Shields, R. (1991) *Places On the Margin*. London: Routledge.

Shivers, J.S. and deLisle, L.J. (1997) *The Story of Leisure: Context, Concepts and Current Controversy*. Leeds: Human Kinetics.

Siisiäinen, M. (2000) 'Two Concepts of Social Capital: Bourdieu versus Putnam'. Paper presented a the ISTR Fourth International Conference 'The Third Sector: For What and For Whom?' Trinity College Dublin, July 5–8.

Simmons, J. (2005) 'IKEA – Brand Of Many', *The Observer*, 12th June.

Skeggs, B. (2009) 'Haunted by the Spectre of Judgement: Respectability, Value and Affect in Class Relations', in K.P. Sveinsson (ed.) *Who Cares about the White Working Class?* Runnymede Trust.

Slater, D. (1998) 'Work/Leisure', in Chris Jenks (ed.) *Core Sociological Dichotomies*. London: Sage.

Spink, J. (1994) *Leisure and the Environment*. Oxford: Butterworth-Heinemann.

Spracklen, K. (2009) *The Meaning and Purpose of Leisure: Habermas and Leisure at the End of Modernity*. Basingstoke: Palgrave Macmillan.

Stallybrass, P. and White, A. (1986) *The Politics and Poetics of Transgression*. London: Methuen.

Stebbins, R.A. (1992) *Amateurs, Professionals and Serious Leisure*. London: McGill-Queen's University Press.

—— (1997) 'Serious Leisure and Wellbeing', in J.T. Haworth, *Work, Leisure and Wellbeing*. London: Routledge, 117–30.

—— (1999) 'Serious Leisure', in T.L. Burton and E.L. Jackson (eds) *Leisure Studies: Prospects for the Twenty-First Century*. State College, PA: Venture Publishing.

—— (2006) *Serious Leisure: A Perspective for our Time*. New Brunswick, New Jersey: Aldine/Transaction.

Stephenson, M.L. and Hughes, H.L. (2005) 'Racialised Boundaries in Tourism and Travel: A Case Study of the UK Black Caribbean Community', *Leisure Studies*, 24 (2): 137–60.

Tawney, R.H. (1958) 'Foreword', in Weber, M. (1930) *The Protestant Ethic and the Spirit of Capitalism*. New York: Charles Scribner's Sons.

Thomas, K. (2009) *The Ends of Life: Roads to Fulfilment in the Early Modern Age*. Oxford: Oxford University Press.

Thompson, E.P. (1967) 'Time, Work Discipline and Industrial Capitalism', *Past and Present*, 38: 56–97.

—— (1968) *The Making of the English Working Class*. Harmondsworth: Penguin.

Thompson, G. (1981) 'Holidays', in *Popular Culture and Everyday Life*. Milton Keynes: Open University Press.

Tomalin, C. (2008) 'The Devils Advocate', *The Guardian Review*, 1st March.

Turner, B.S. (1984) *Body and Society*. Oxford: Blackwell.

Turner, V.W. (1973) 'The Center Out There: Pilgrim's Goal', *History of Religions*, 12 (3): 191–230.

Veal, A.J. (1989) 'Leisure, Lifestyle and Status: A Pluralist Framework for Analysis', *Leisure Studies*, 8 (2): 141–53.

—— (1992) 'Definitions of Leisure and Recreation', *Australian Journal of Leisure and Recreation*, 2 (4): 44–8, 52, Republished by School of Leisure, Sport and Tourism, University of Technology, Sydney, as Working Paper No. 4, accessed at: www.business.uts.edu.au/lst/research on 18th July, 2008.

—— (2001) 'Leisure, Culture and Lifestyle', *Loisir et Société/Society and Leisure*, 24 (2): 359–76.

Veblen, T. (1934 1899) *Theory of the Leisure Class: An Economic Study in the Evolution of Institutions*. New York: Modern Library.

von Weizäcker, C. F. (1988) *The Ambivalence of Progress*. New York: Paragon House Publishers.

Wacquant, L. (1998) 'Pierre Bourdeu', in R. Stones (ed.) *Key Sociological Thinkers*. Basingstoke: Macmillan.

Walton, J.K. and Walvin, J. (eds) (1983) *Leisure in Britain 1780–1939*. Manchester: Manchester University Press.

Wearing, B. (1998) *Leisure and Feminist Theory*. London: Sage.

Webb, J., Schirato, T. and Danaher, G. (2002) *Understanding Bourdieu*. London: Sage.

Weber, M. (1930) *The Protestant Ethic and the Spirit of Capitalism*. London: Unwin Hyman Ltd.

Wellman, B., Carrington, P. and Hall, A. (1988) 'Networks as Personal Communities', in B. Wellman and S. Berkowitz (eds) *Social Structures: A Network Approach*. Cambridge: Cambridge University Press.

Wheaton, B. (ed.) (2004) *Understanding Lifestyle Sports: Consumption, Identity and Difference*. Abingdon: Routledge.

Williams, B. (1993) *Shame and Necessity*. Berkeley, CA: University of California Press.

Williams, R. (1961) 'Work and Leisure', in *The Listener*, 25th May, 926–7.

—— (1973) *The Country and the City*. London: Chatto & Windus.

Wittgenstein, L. (1967) *Philosophical Investigations*. Oxford: Blackwell.

—— (1993) *Philosophical Occasions, 1912–1951*. Edited by James Klagge and Alfred Nordmann. Indianapolis, IN: Hackett Publishing Company, Inc.

Wollen, P. (2007) 'On Gaze Theory', *New Left Review*, 44 (March/April): 91–106.

Žižek, S. (1989) *The Sublime Object of Ideology*. London: Verso.

INDEX